ATASCOSA
BANDERA
BASTROP
BELL
BEXAR
CALDWELL
COMAL
COMANCHE
CORYELL
FALLS
GRIMES
GUADALUPE
HAMILTON
HAYS
HILL
LEON
LIMESTONE
LLANO
MCCULLOCH
MCLENNAN
NAVARRO
REAL
ROBERTSON
SAN SABA
TRAVIS

BLANCO
BOSQUE
BRAZOS
BURLESON
BURNET
FAYETTE
FREESTONE
FRIO
GILLESPIE
GONZALES
KARNES
KENDALL
KERR
LAMPASAS
LEE
MADISON
MASON
MEDINA
MILAM
MILLS
UVALDE
WASHINGTON
WILLIAMSON
WILSON
ZAVALA

Wilson County Courthouse, 1884, Floresville, Texas

NUMBER TWENTY

Clifton and Shirley Caldwell Texas Heritage Series

THE COURTHOUSES OF CENTRAL TEXAS

The Courthouses of Central Texas

BRANTLEY HIGHTOWER

University of Texas Press
AUSTIN

Publication of this work was made possible in part by support from Clifton and Shirley Caldwell and a challenge grant from the National Endowment for the Humanities.

Printed in Singapore
First edition, 2015

♾ The paper used in this book meets the minimum requirements of ANSI/NISO Z39.48-1992 (R1997) (Permanence of Paper).

LIBRARY OF CONGRESS CATALOGING-IN-PUBLICATION DATA

Hightower, Brantley, 1976-
The courthouses of central Texas / Brantley Hightower. — First edition.
pages cm. — (Clifton and Shirley Caldwell Texas heritage series ; number 20)
Includes bibliographical references and index.
ISBN 978-0-292-76294-7 (cloth : alk. paper)
1. Courthouses—Texas. 2. Texas—History. I. Title.
NA4472.T4H54 2015
725'.1509764—dc23 2014017583

doi:10.7560/762947

Photo, pp. vi–vii, Bexar County Courthouse, 1896, San Antonio, Texas.
Photo, pp. xiv–xv, McLennan County Courthouse, 1901, Waco, Texas.
Unless otherwise noted, all photographs, illustrations, and charts are by the author.

FOR SAMMY, OF COURSE.

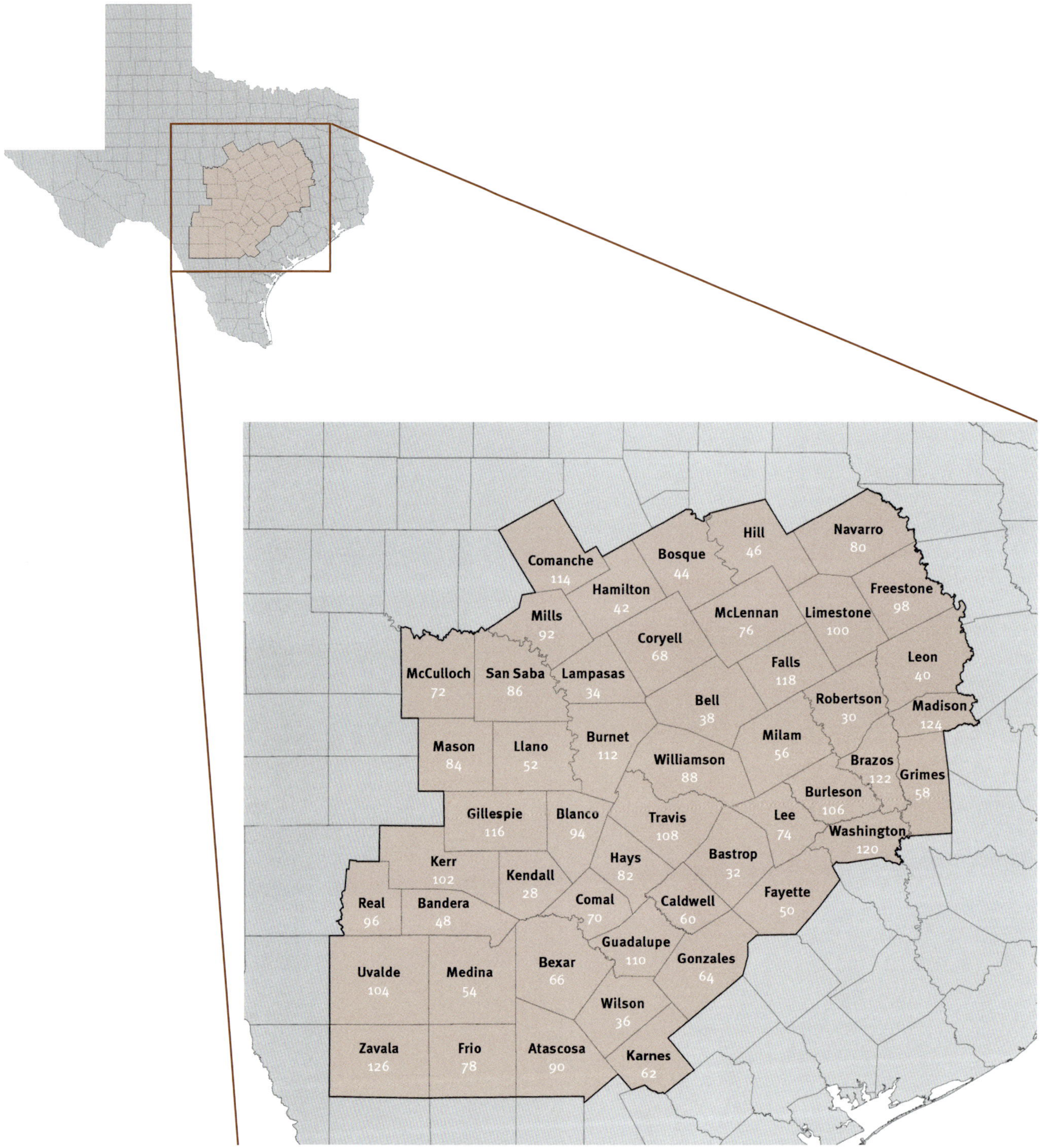
Comanche
114
Hill
46
Navarro
80
Bosque
44
Hamilton
42
Freestone
98
Mills
92
McLennan
76
Limestone
100
Coryell
68
Leon
40
Falls
118
McCulloch
72
San Saba
86
Lampasas
34
Bell
38
Robertson
30
Madison
124
Burnet
112
Milam
56
Mason
84
Llano
52
Williamson
88
Brazos
122
Grimes
58
Burleson
106
Gillespie
116
Blanco
94
Travis
108
Lee
74
Washington
120
Hays
82
Bastrop
32
Kerr
102
Kendall
28
Fayette
50
Caldwell
60
Real
96
Bandera
48
Comal
70
Guadalupe
110
Bexar
66
Gonzales
64
Uvalde
104
Medina
54
Wilson
36
Zavala
126
Frio
78
Atascosa
90
Karnes
62

Contents

Bosque County Courthouse, 1886, Meridian, Texas

Foreword

Driving through central Texas, one may occasionally see a lone, noble tree standing out in a field. Strangely, despite one's speed in passing, something of this tree's rings can be sensed: the tree's narrow years and luxurious years; tractor scars and lightning strikes; its leaf-rustling sanctuary; the human deference it has taken for it to survive in that spot; its role as a point of orientation for ranchers, critters, and passersby; the way it marks the passage of time. All these things we somehow instantly register, consciously or not. Perhaps this awareness arises from some primitive instinct, or maybe from childhood rambles when our perceptions were new and literally closer to the ground.

Drive on farther and another scene may be encountered: a lone, noble building standing in a town's clearing, one of the fifty county courthouses included in this book. As with those venerable trees, the life stories of these buildings are embodied in their weathered forms: their narrow and luxurious years; their wounds from lightning and the human equivalent thereof; the echo in their halls; the human deference that has allowed these buildings to endure; their role as points of orientation, as centers staked in wide country, officiating over the passage of time. But unlike our innate sensitivity to the trees' stories, we are less well attuned to the voices of buildings.

This remarkable book sensitizes us to what these courthouses have to say. Brantley Hightower's harvest of keen observation and his unusual way of depicting it graphically allow us an intense view of a subject never before assembled in this way. Untainted by nostalgia, his work broadens our thinking. Between the lines the reader may discern truths about Texas, about courthouse justice for some folks and injustice for others, and certain fundamentals about urban design and the unraveling of cities today. What also emerges is this architectural principle: that a single building, distinguished by its setting and composure, crafted with care and designed with meaning for its community, can affect an entire town. Such buildings invite us to care about them, and then to literally care for them, so that they endure longer than other buildings, and even outlive ourselves.

Our forebears encountered a wild natural landscape. They built primarily for physical shelter. A little later on they added shelter for the eye and the mind and the heart, like these courthouses, which civilized town and countryside for miles around. Today we encounter a landscape of manmade wildness. Physical shelter we have pretty well in hand, but buildings for the eye, mind, and heart that can tame the mess we have created around us are rare indeed. The buildings in this book are quietly instructive in this regard.

Texans have long come over the rise and seen the courthouse silhouette up ahead. That image is always somehow reassuring, even though most of us today know these buildings only as passing acquaintances. How good it is to deepen these acquaintances after all these years.

MAX LEVY, FAIA   DALLAS, TEXAS   OCTOBER 2013

THE COURTHOUSES OF CENTRAL TEXAS

Lockhart, Texas

Introduction

In the summer of 1955 two men newly appointed to the University of Texas architecture faculty took advantage of the pause in their teaching responsibilities to explore the area around their new Austin home. In their travels through central Texas they discovered a landscape of small towns containing buildings of surprising architectural sophistication. The experience made an impression on them both, and later they would describe their observations in *Architectural Record* magazine.[1] In "Lockhart, Texas" they depict the central Texas town featured in the essay as an urban model worthy of detailed study. Like many small towns in America, it was inspired by European architectural and urban precedents, but in the case of Lockhart they saw a distinctly Texan approach. For the authors, the county courthouse and its square held particular interest:

For these courthouse squares are not the residential enclosures of England, nor like the piazzas of Italy do they admit the church in a presiding role. Here it is the law which assumes a public significance; and it is around the secular image of the law, like architectural illustrations of a political principal, that these towns revolve. In each case the courthouse is both visual focus and social guarantee; and in each square the reality of government made formally explicit provides the continuing assurance of order.[2]

The two young architecture professors who made these observations were Colin Rowe and John Hejduk, who both became influential architectural theorists and educators in the second half of the twentieth century. Their fascination with the seat of Caldwell County attests to the powerful allure of courthouses and the towns in which they reside.

The 254 county courthouses of Texas represent a diverse expression of the idealized values and ambitions of a rapidly expanding population during times of intense economic, technological, and social change. The courthouses of the central part of the state provide an illustrative sample of the larger forces at work throughout Texas. In the century during which the first and last existent central Texas county courthouses were constructed, the state expanded from a mostly untamed wilderness of under 820,000 inhabitants to a modern center of business and technology with a population of over 11 million.[3] Today that number is over 26 million. When the Kendall County Courthouse opened in 1870, Comanche war parties and roving bands of outlaws were still a reality in Texas. Courthouse buildings by themselves did not end these threats, but the institutional services and legal protections provided by the county government they contained did much to establish a stable civil society.

Counties are required by the Texas Constitution to build courthouse facilities to house the departments that define government at that level. Functionally they have always been office buildings with archive storage and clerical space in addition to a few specialized courtroom facilities. Early courthouses were built as pragmatic containers of program, but by the closing decades of the 1800s, the courthouse began to be understood as a potent symbol of a community's prosperity. County governments would invest far beyond their means in a bold architecture of optimism whose aspirational grandiosity illustrated the future they envisioned for themselves and their people. Of course, this vision was the exclusive domain of the county's white property owners. A courthouse could just as easily be a symbol of corruption and injustice for the less privileged members of the community.

As Texas became more densely settled and the rule of law became more institutionally entrenched, county government became a less central fixture in the daily life of the average citizen. The courthouses built during this

Caldwell County Courthouse, 1894, Lockhart, Texas

transitional period reflect this changing reality. Although the relative importance of county government continued to wane as the state became increasingly urbanized, the "temples of justice" that were built in its name still serve as vivid reminders of how significant the county once was to Texans.

The frontier may have been civilized long ago, but courthouses still provide a way to better understand a time and an attitude toward architecture and government that was radically different from the one that exists today. What is more, they provide a compelling example of the importance of architecture in the public realm.

CENTRAL TEXAS

The vast physical size of Texas means that the state encompasses a wide variety of geographic and climatic regions within its boundaries. It consists of rolling prairies to the north, piney woods to the east, coastal plains to the south, and mountains and basins to the west, with rugged hill country in its middle. The central area of the state presents a unique convergence of these varied regions. The area also includes an equally diverse cultural sampling of Anglo, Czech, German, and Mexican cultures.[4] While the confluence of these influences defined the history of the state as a

Freestone County Courthouse, 1919, Fairfield, Texas

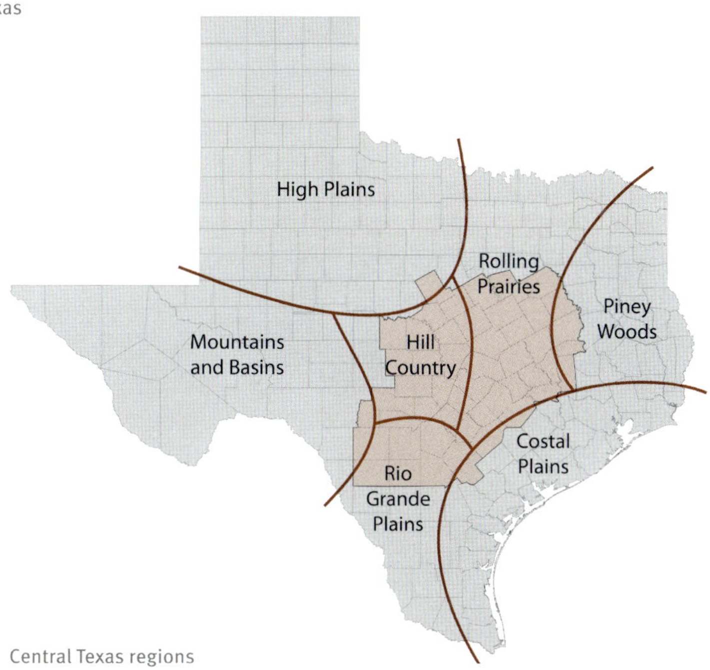

Central Texas regions

Mason County Courthouse, 1909, Mason, Texas

Williamson County Courthouse, 1911, Georgetown, Texas

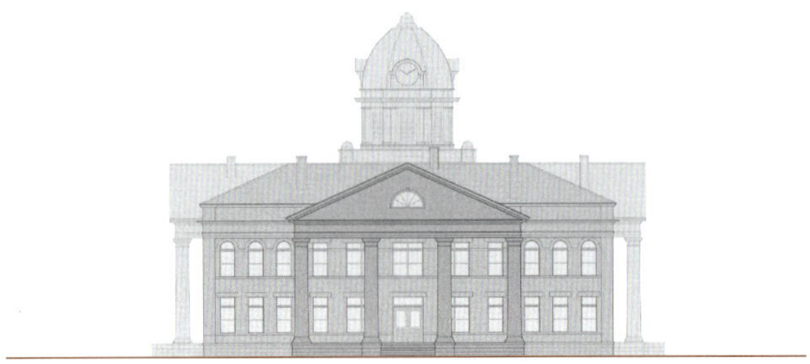

Mason County Courthouse, 1909, Mason, Texas

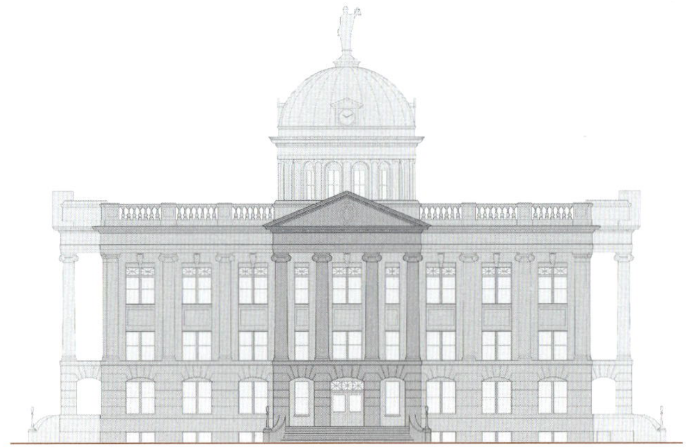

Williamson County Courthouse, 1911, Georgetown, Texas

whole, in central Texas it also determined its architecture. It was not uncommon for limestone quarried in the hill country to be worked by skilled German immigrants who created forms influenced by Hispanic precedent.

PROCESS

The creation of consistently scaled and formatted architectural drawings allows the direct comparison of courthouse buildings in a way never before possible. Courthouses that appear similar when viewed in isolation reveal themselves to be radically different in scale or density of ornamentation when rendered adjacent to one another.

Every attempt has been made to create an accurate portrait of the courthouses studied. Each courthouse was photographed and measured when it was visited on multiple occasions over the course of several years. When possible, existing architectural drawings were used to verify field measurements.[5]

Deciding what to draw was not always obvious. Counties often expanded their facilities incrementally over time,

2012 photo of Robertson County Courthouse, 1882, Franklin, Texas

2013 photo of Robertson County Courthouse, 1882, Franklin, Texas

2014 photo of Robertson County Courthouse, 1882, Franklin, Texas

resulting in courthouse squares littered with buildings of different eras and purposes. In some cases large new annexes were built that dwarfed the original structure they were constructed to support. For this study, a county's earliest functioning courthouse was drawn. Additions were included, but stand-alone annexes were not. Certain additive details such as air conditioning units, downspouts, and handrails have been omitted for analytical clarity.

It is worth noting that these buildings are dynamic entities whose appearances can change dramatically over time. During the research phase of this project, several courthouses underwent extensive restorations and appear significantly different than when the study began. As such, the drawings and photographs assembled here can best be understood as a single snapshot of a specific time in a continuing evolution.

Grimes County Courthouse, 1893, Anderson, Texas

The County Courthouse

For most of its history, Texas was a rural state. In an economy dominated by a combination of farming and ranching, small towns served as important commercial centers within a larger agricultural landscape. Even as the rest of the country urbanized and saw a corresponding shift in political and cultural power to urban centers, in Texas the small town remained the dominant urban form until the middle part of the twentieth century.[1] Since municipal governments were minimal, and as the presence of the federal government was limited, the county was by default the most visible level of government for many Texans. Although counties exist as extensions of state government, county officials are locally elected and by design do not answer directly to anyone at the state or federal level.[2]

The collection of county courthouses built in central Texas represents a wide spectrum of architectural styles, approaches, and ambitions. This diversity is not random, but the product of the specific social, economic, and political forces in existence when a courthouse was designed and constructed. As such, each courthouse can be seen as a reflection of a particular community at a particular place and time.

THE COUNTY

When Texas became an independent republic in 1836, it converted the preexisting Mexican governmental districts into twenty-three counties to serve the newly formed nation. These counties would become the administrative arms of the state of Texas when it was annexed to the United States a decade later.[3] In the years that followed, new counties were carved out of existing ones as the population of a particular area grew to a point that a new county government was warranted. The current total of 254 was reached in 1921.

To the contemporary Texan, the county can seem like an arbitrary and invisible political division. Unless a county border follows the course of a river, one of its only physical manifestations is the change in pavement type that occurs where one county's road maintenance ends and another's begins. In addition to constructing and maintaining its road infrastructure, Texas counties are empowered to operate a jail and judicial system, collect taxes, and preserve important records. The county also provides law enforce-

Bell County Courthouse, 1884, Belton, Texas

Leon County Courthouse, 1886, Centerville, Texas

Comanche County line

Gonzales, Texas, seat of Gonzales County

ment protection and issues various licenses and registrations to the general population. It does not operate public schools or utilities as counties do in some other states.[4] Texas counties originally raised revenue exclusively through property taxes, but this income source has since been augmented with the addition of sales taxes, use fees, permitting fees, and fines.

Although each county government is tasked with the same functions, the scale at which each must operate varies widely. Brewster County, the largest in the state, encompasses 6,193 square miles and is larger than the state of Connecticut. Rockwall County, the smallest, consists of only 149 square miles. Even more extreme is the variation in population. Home to the Houston metropolitan area, Harris County has a population of almost 4.1 million, while Loving County has but eighty-two inhabitants.

To accommodate such wildly varying county sizes and populations, the Texas Legislature established a court system with a complex geographic and subject matter framework. This has resulted in a judicial network that, although consistent in purpose, appears convoluted in execution. For example, district courts in Texas are the state's trial courts of general jurisdiction. They have exclusive authority in felony cases, but their authority over civil cases may overlap with the county courts', depending on the district in question. A single district court may have a jurisdiction that spans several counties in less populated areas, while multiple district courts may exist in more populated urban centers.

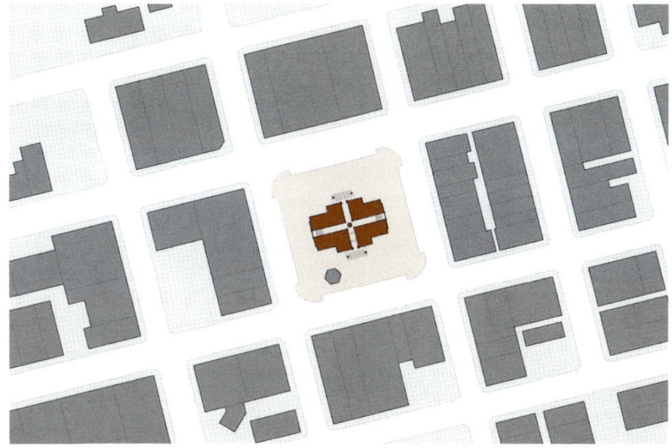

Brenham, Texas, seat of Washington County

Fredericksburg, Texas, seat of Gillespie County

THE COUNTY SEAT

The "Laws of the Indies" were a broad range of decrees issued by the Spanish Crown over the course of several hundred years, beginning in the sixteenth century. These laws sought to define how Spain's far-flung colonies would be structured, maintained, and governed. Regarding town planning, they called for the creation of a central plaza with the local church and government buildings forming its perimeter. Remnants of these early urban planning efforts can still be seen in the centers of Spanish land grant towns, such as Gonzales.

Most towns in Texas came into existence well after Spain had ceased to control Texas, but although this meant more freedom was available when it came to the layout of new towns, urban planning expertise was not readily available on the frontier. As a result, town founders typically

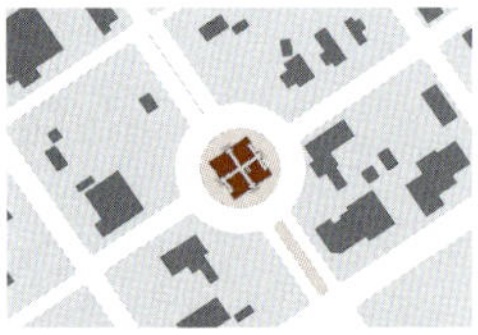
ATASCOSA

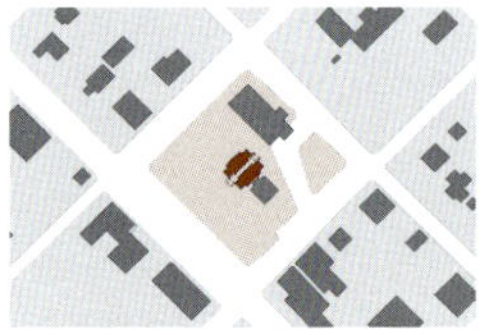
BANDERA

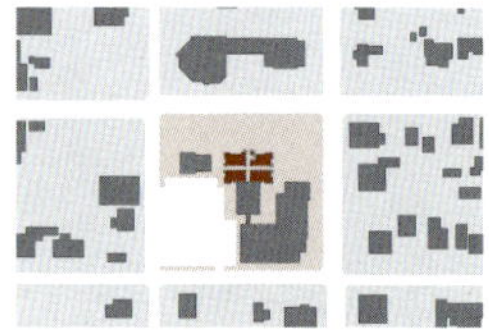
BASTROP

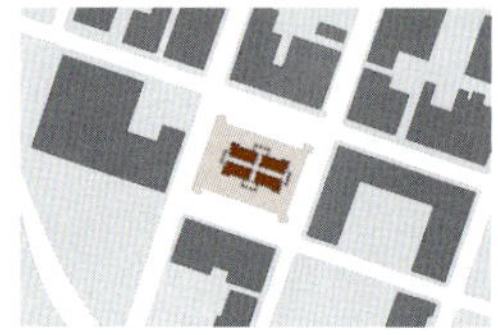
BELL

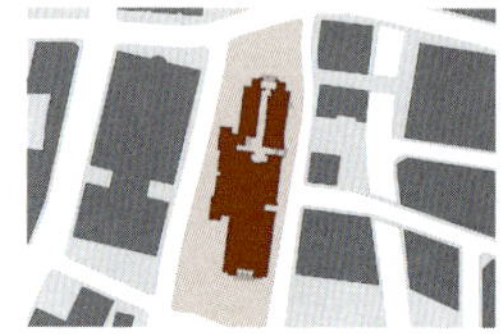
BEXAR

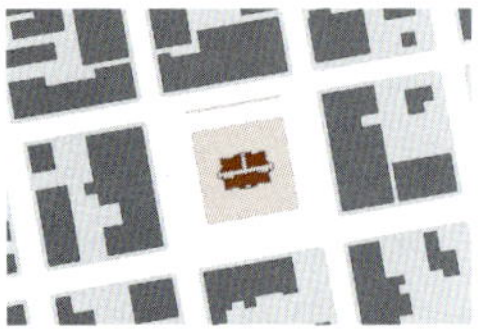
CALDWELL

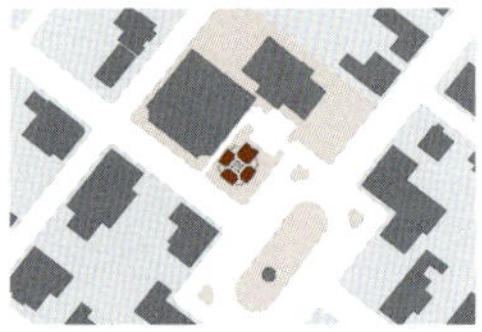
COMAL

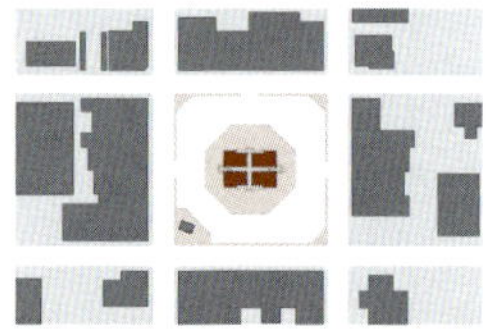
COMANCHE

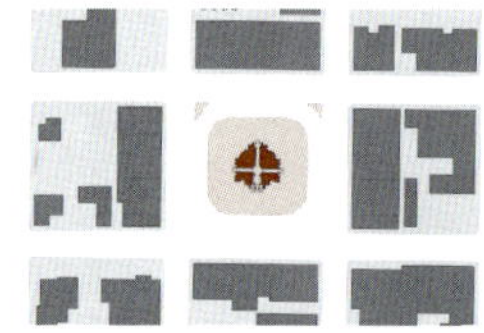
CORYELL

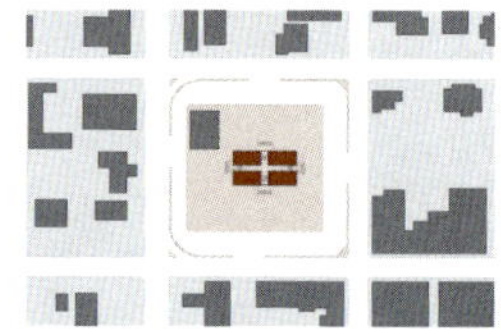
FALLS

GRIMES

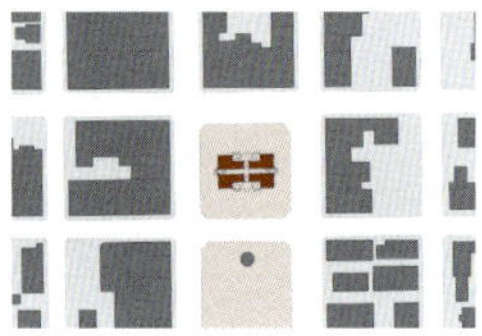
GUADALUPE

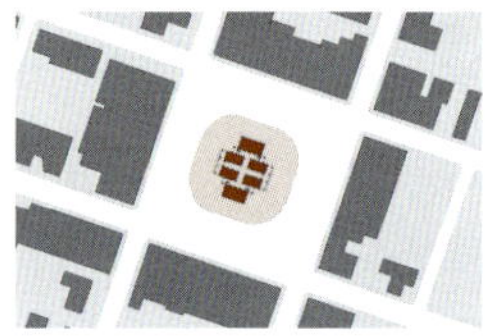
HAMILTON

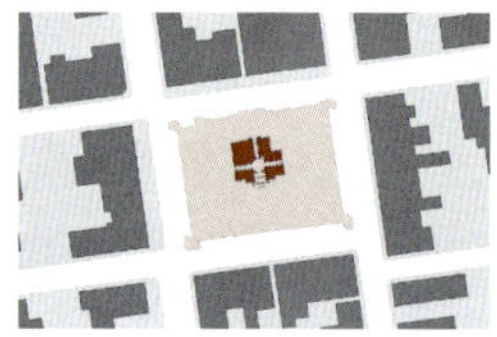
HAYS

HILL

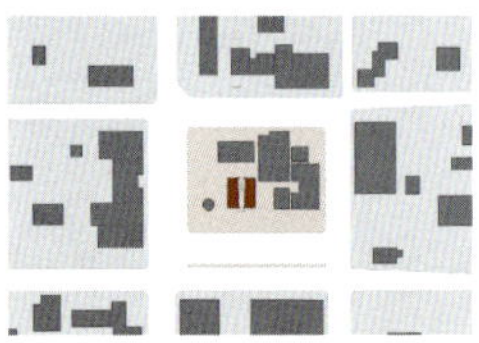
LEON

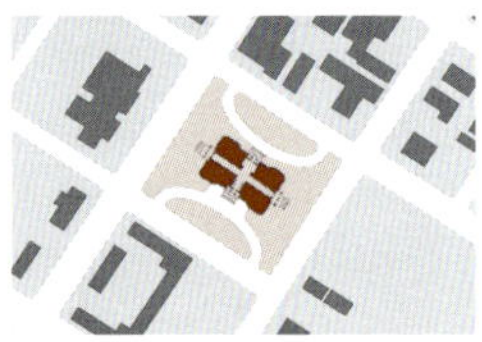
LIMESTONE

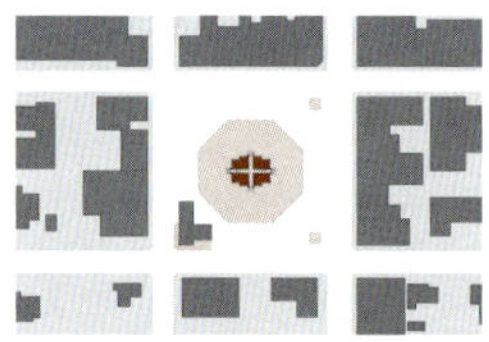
LLANO

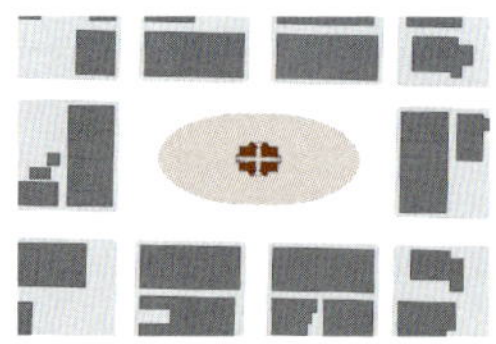
MCCULLOCH

MCLENNAN

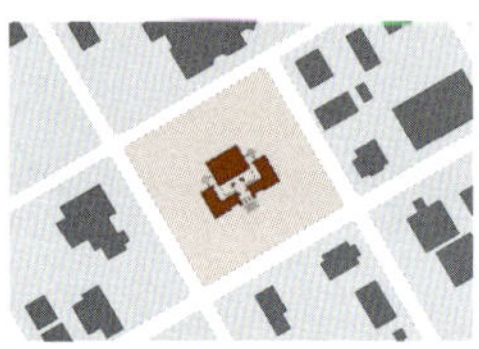
NAVARRO

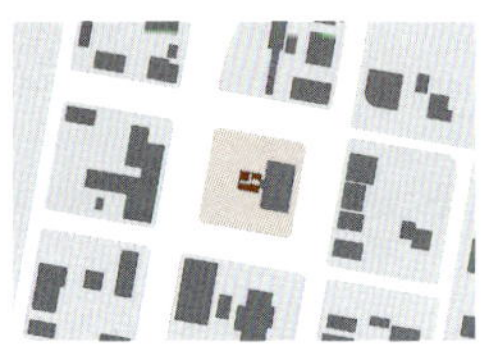
REAL

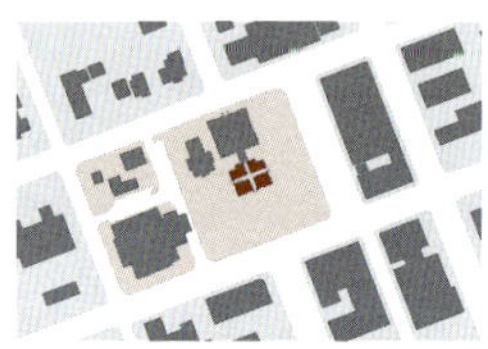
ROBERTSON

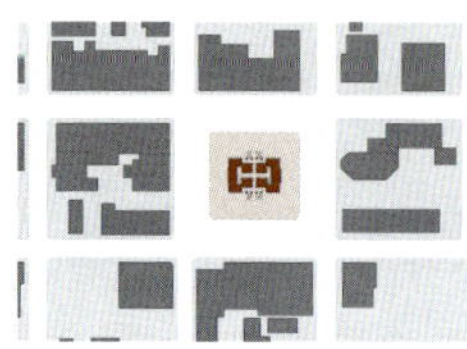
SAN SABA

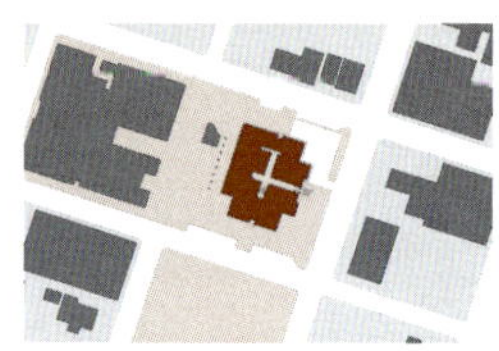
TRAVIS

resorted to importing familiar planning models from their particular places of origin.[5] Towns established by Anglo settlers tended to delineate strict grid plans with limited public space, while those settled by immigrants from continental Europe were much more generous with their allocation of communal land.[6]

Because courthouses drew visitors from the entirety of a county, they also functioned as economic anchors for the towns in which they came to reside. The designation of a town as a county seat would not only ensure the town's survival, but often it would also provide the town with the catalyst it needed to become the commercial center of

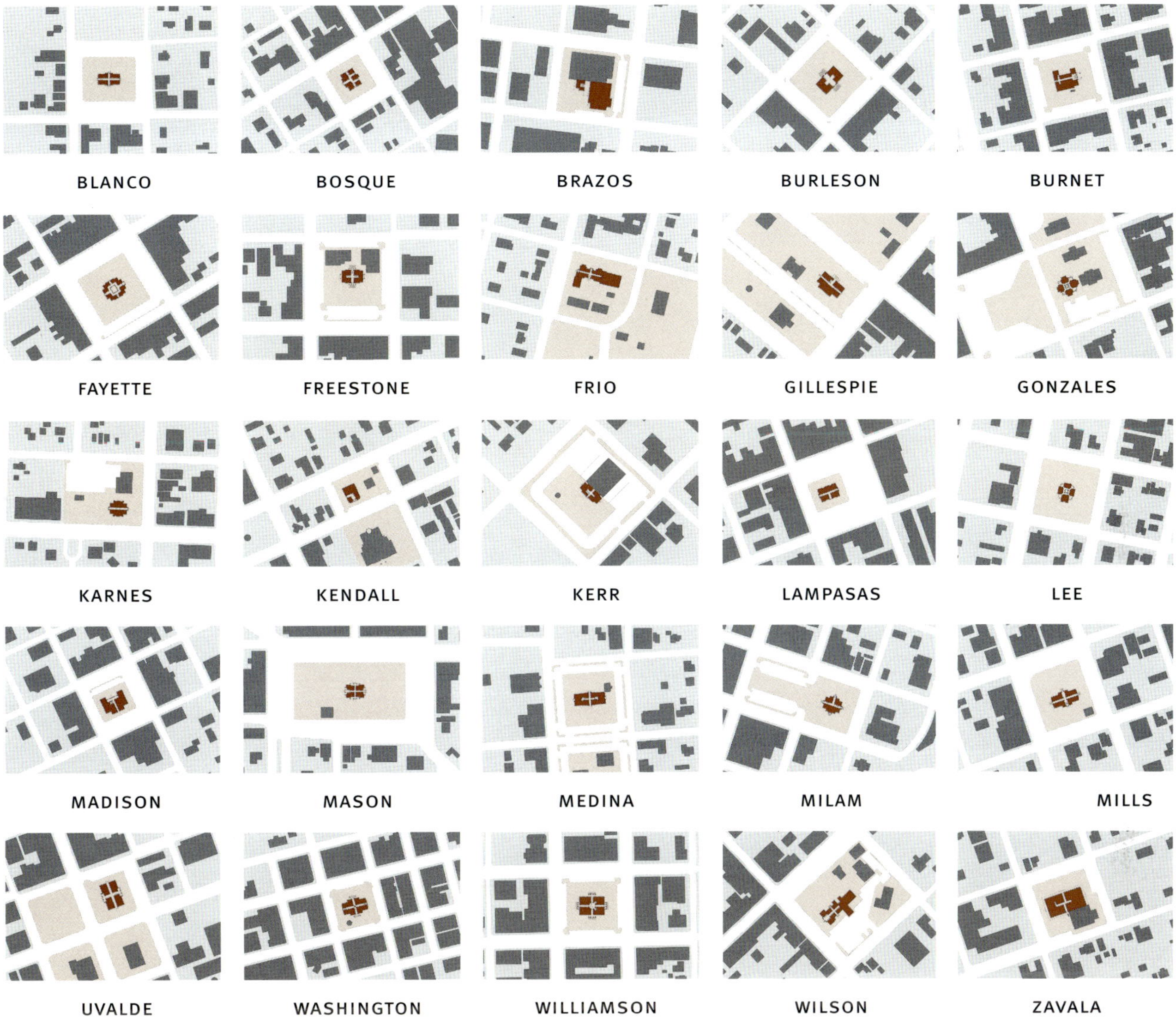

The courthouse squares of central Texas

its region. For this reason the designation of a town as a county seat was a hotly—and at times violently—contested issue. Although state law provided a mechanism by which a county seat could be legally moved, the execution of such an act was often defined by subterfuge, the secretive late night transfer of county records, and occasional gunplay.

San Marcos, Texas, seat of Hays County

Lampasas, Texas, seat of Lampasas County

THE COURTHOUSE SQUARE

The open public plaza that defined the Spanish tradition of town planning is conceptually quite different from the type of courthouse square found throughout central Texas. With a few exceptions, in Texas the courthouse sits in the middle of the public square rather than facing it.[7] The result is that instead of the courthouse acting as a frame for public space, in central Texas the public space acts as a frame for the courthouse.

The size of a courthouse's square varies considerably depending on the grid dimensions of the county seat in which it resides. In central Texas, city blocks range from 440 feet along each side to a mere 160 feet square.[8] The need for increased automobile parking has additionally eroded some squares, rendering some courthouses as isolated buildings floating within a vast sea of asphalt.

Regardless of their size, courthouse squares perform the same basic functions. Often located at the highest elevation in town, they imbue the building they host with a heightened physical prominence. Acting as the public front yard of its community, the land around the courthouse mitigates the scale of the building contained within it. The potentially domineering presence of the courthouse is thus rendered more approachable and humane. The square's placement in the town's commercial center also ensures that it is integrated into the daily life of the town. Fully developed commercial districts around courthouse squares are often found in towns that flourished at the end of the nineteenth century when development was focused around the courthouse.[9] If a town's growth occurred after the turn of the twentieth century and the advent of the automobile, retail development was more likely to be located along a commercial strip on the highways leading into town.

No matter how small the county seat, every county courthouse in central Texas exists within an urban context. Several planning strategies were deployed over time to differentiate the courthouse square from adjacent city blocks. The origins of these typologies have been traced to specific towns in Tennessee, Virginia, and Pennsylvania. The names of these towns can be used to help identify the individual strategies they represent.[10]

SHELBYVILLE SQUARE—*A single block is designated as the site of the county's courthouse within a regular gridiron of streets. This is the most prevalent square type in Texas.*

HARRISONBURG SQUARE—*The courthouse square can also be shifted relative to the predominant street grid, placing the county courthouse on axis with the town's main street.*

Hill County Courthouse square, Hillsboro, Texas

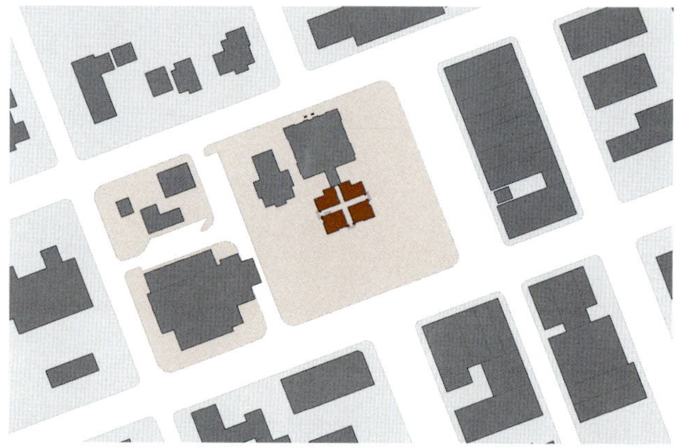

Robertson County Courthouse square, Franklin, Texas

Hillsboro, Texas

Franklin, Texas

LANCASTER SQUARE—*The courthouse square can be shifted a half block in two directions, resulting in the placement of the courthouse at the intersection of two streets.*

TWO-BLOCK SQUARE—*This type of square is formed by the amalgamation of two city blocks to create a larger setting for the courthouse, allowing it to function more like a park.*

Atascosa County Courthouse square, Jourdanton, Texas

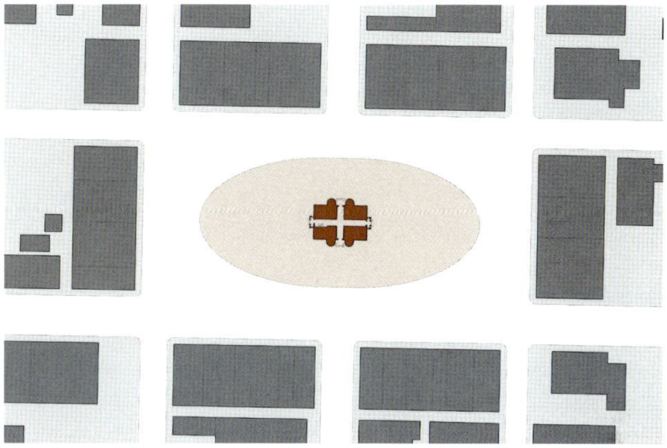

McCulloch County Courthouse square, Brady, Texas

Jourdanton, Texas

Brady, Texas

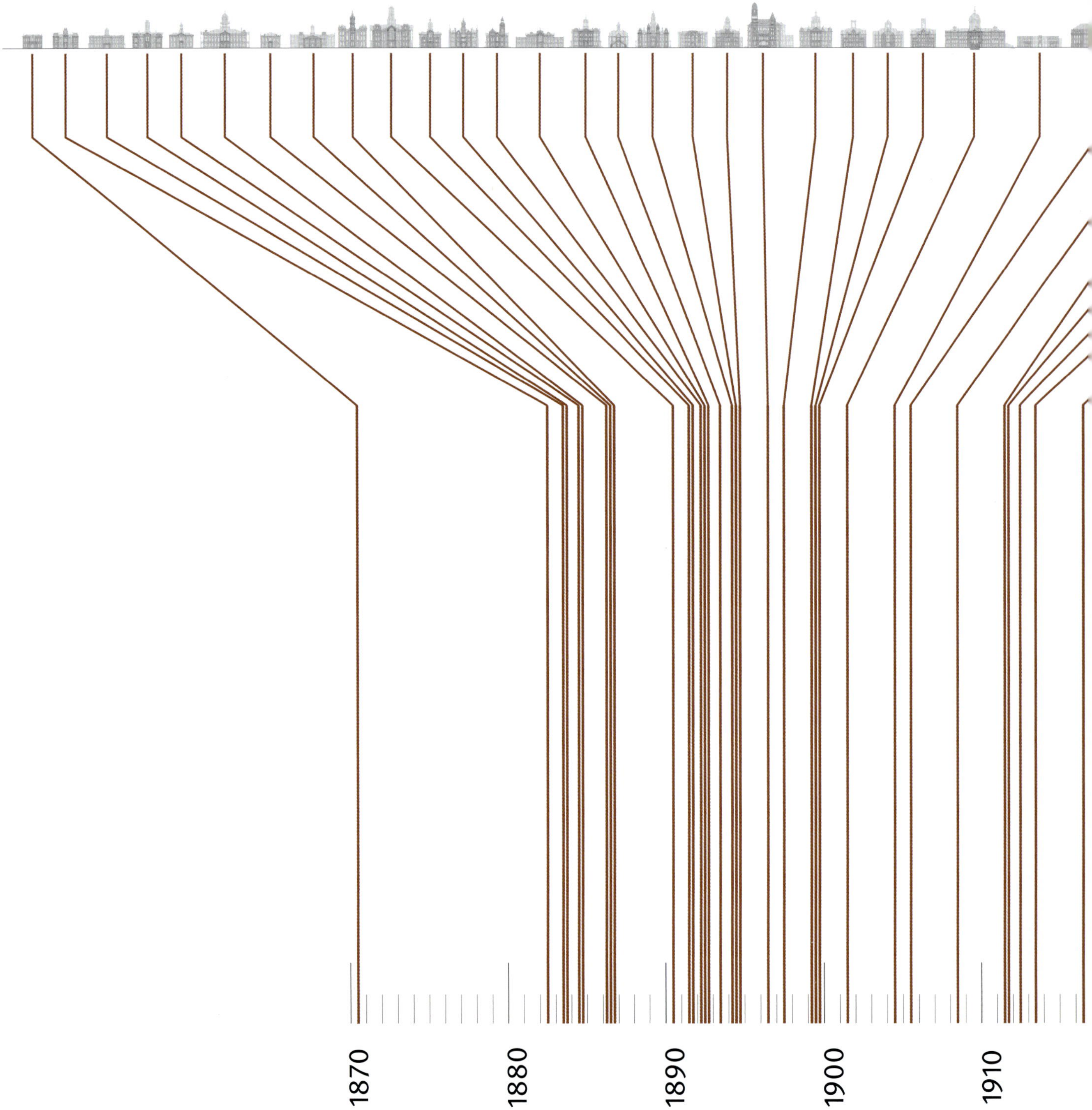
1870
1880
1890
1900
1910

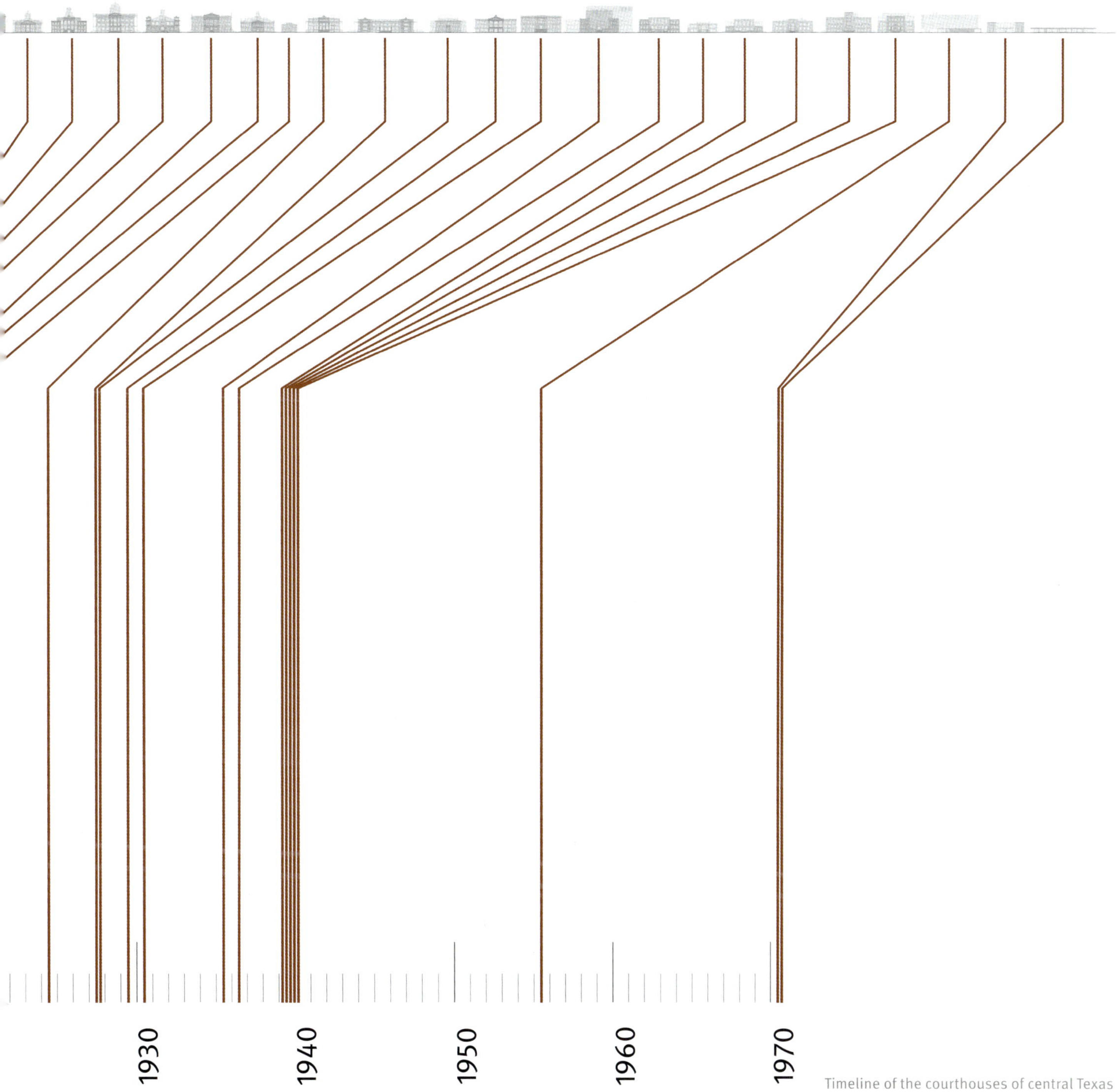

Timeline of the courthouses of central Texas

THE COURTHOUSE BUILDING

County courthouse buildings are incongruous architectural artifacts. They are at once both monumental and approachable. They relate to their immediate context even as they set themselves apart as singular architectural landmarks. They symbolize abstract ideas about self-governance while also fulfilling mundane functional needs. A courthouse provides a direct physical interface between county government and the people it serves while acting as a formal backdrop for both the social and political events of a community.[11]

Every one of the fifty courthouses of central Texas was built in the one hundred years between 1870 and 1970. All but four of these buildings were constructed within the much shorter period between 1882 and 1939. These fifty-seven years saw a series of courthouse building booms that corresponded to the availability of alternative funding options provided by both the state and federal governments.

Over the course of their individual histories, counties typically constructed multiple courthouse buildings.[12] Larger and more substantial edifices would in time replace early utilitarian structures. The first courthouse built by a county would often be a simple structure intended to meet the immediate needs of a newly established county. These first-generation courthouses were often square in plan with four near-identical façades of wood or simple masonry. Internally these designs consisted of offices on the ground floor, while the second floor was dominated by a single large courtroom space. This basic interior diagram would remain essentially unchanged until the middle part of the twentieth century.

Courthouse design remained quite utilitarian in Texas until after the Civil War. A boom in railroad construction in the 1870s brought with it an influx of immigrants as well as a greater exposure to the latest architectural styles and technologies emanating from the Midwest and East Coast. More importantly, the increased connection to national markets allowed Texas to became a leader in the production of cotton and beef. As their economies expanded, counties collected more in taxes and could make larger investments in the architecture of their courthouses.

Even so, the capital investment needed to design and construct a significant courthouse building was still out of reach for all but the largest and wealthiest counties. This changed in 1874 when a law passed by the Texas Legislature authorized counties to issue bonds to fund the construction of county facilities. This financial apparatus allowed counties to build the larger buildings they needed in the more opulent styles they desired.[13] As a result, counties almost uniformly abandoned the simple cubic massing that defined the exteriors of earlier courthouses in favor of more ornate designs that referenced contemporary architectural trends.

The closing decades of the 1800s represented a golden age of county courthouse construction in central Texas. Counties invested in substantial public buildings of a richness and exuberance that had not been economically feasible before and has not been politically possible since. Although often described as "Victorian," the architecture associated with this era is diverse. The catchall term broadly refers to the picturesque massing and ornate detailing that defined architecture in Europe during the reign of Queen Victoria, but in Texas it more specifically refers to a sequence of stylistic revivals that architects used in the closing decades of the nineteenth century. The Italianate, Second Empire, and Romanesque styles were all used extensively throughout central Texas.

The eclecticism of this approach represented an ideal solution to the question of style for the county courthouse. Even when a specific historical reference was used as a point of departure, the architect of the 1880s and 1890s had the freedom to develop that style into a personal expression. This flexibility also allowed neighboring counties to construct courthouses that possessed distinctive identities even if they were quite similar in size and layout. Built of locally available building materials, these imported styles were imbued with a distinctly Texan flavor when rendered in white limestone and pink granite.[14]

Almost always bilaterally symmetrical, the courthouse of this era had façades that were divided into a number of smaller articulated pavilions, reducing the building's overall mass.[15] As with previous designs, four exterior entrances led to two intersecting interior corridors that provided access to county offices located on the ground floor. The courthouse's second level was dominated by the building's double-height district courtroom and was flanked by various support spaces. Occupying the full width of the building, this courtroom space received natural light and ventilation from windows located on two or more sides.

By the dawn of the twentieth century, the stylistic influence of the World's Columbian Exposition of 1893 arrived in Texas, bringing with it a more formal approach to town planning and architectural design. With the exposition's references to Roman precedent, the monumental columns and domes of classical architecture became the consensus style for public buildings in Texas. Whereas earlier courthouses sought to emphasize the vertical through the proportional distortion of architectural elements and details, these new designs sought to replicate classical proportions and details.[16] Internally, these courthouses became increasingly complex, with arrangements that allowed for the addition of secondary courtroom spaces within the same traditional planning model.

Towers and domes have historically been used to signify the importance of the buildings located beneath them. Because of the relative flatness of the Texas landscape, these elements could often be visible for miles. They served practical needs as well. As hot air rises within a building, it collects in the uppermost volumes of the structure. If that structure is designed with an operable lantern or cupola, this warmer, lighter air can be exhausted outside while cooler, heavier air is drawn in through open windows on the lower floors. The effectiveness of this upward

Leon County Courthouse, 1886, Centerville, Texas

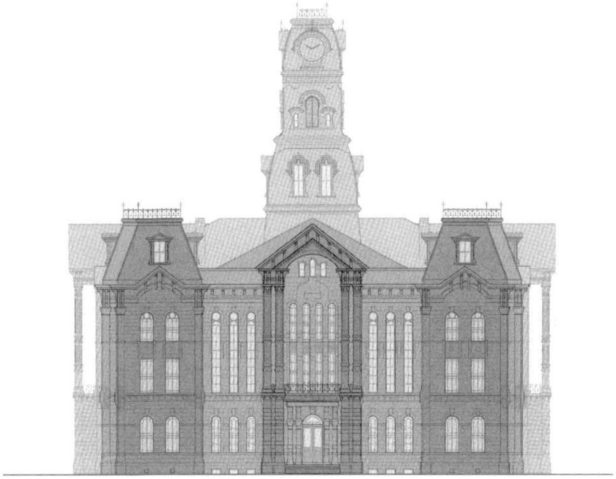

Hill County Courthouse, 1890, Hillsboro, Texas

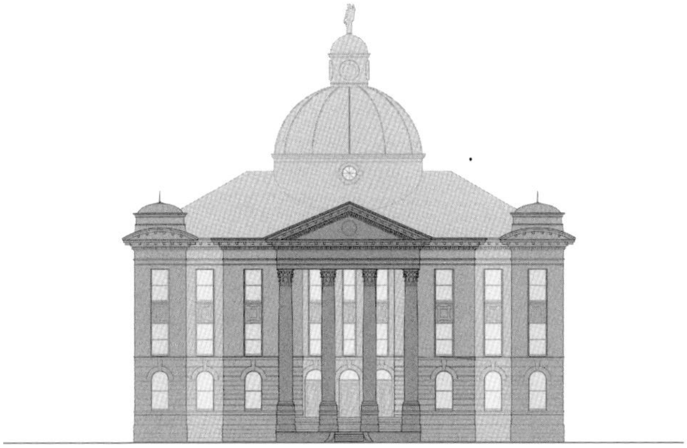

Hays County Courthouse, 1908, San Marcos, Texas

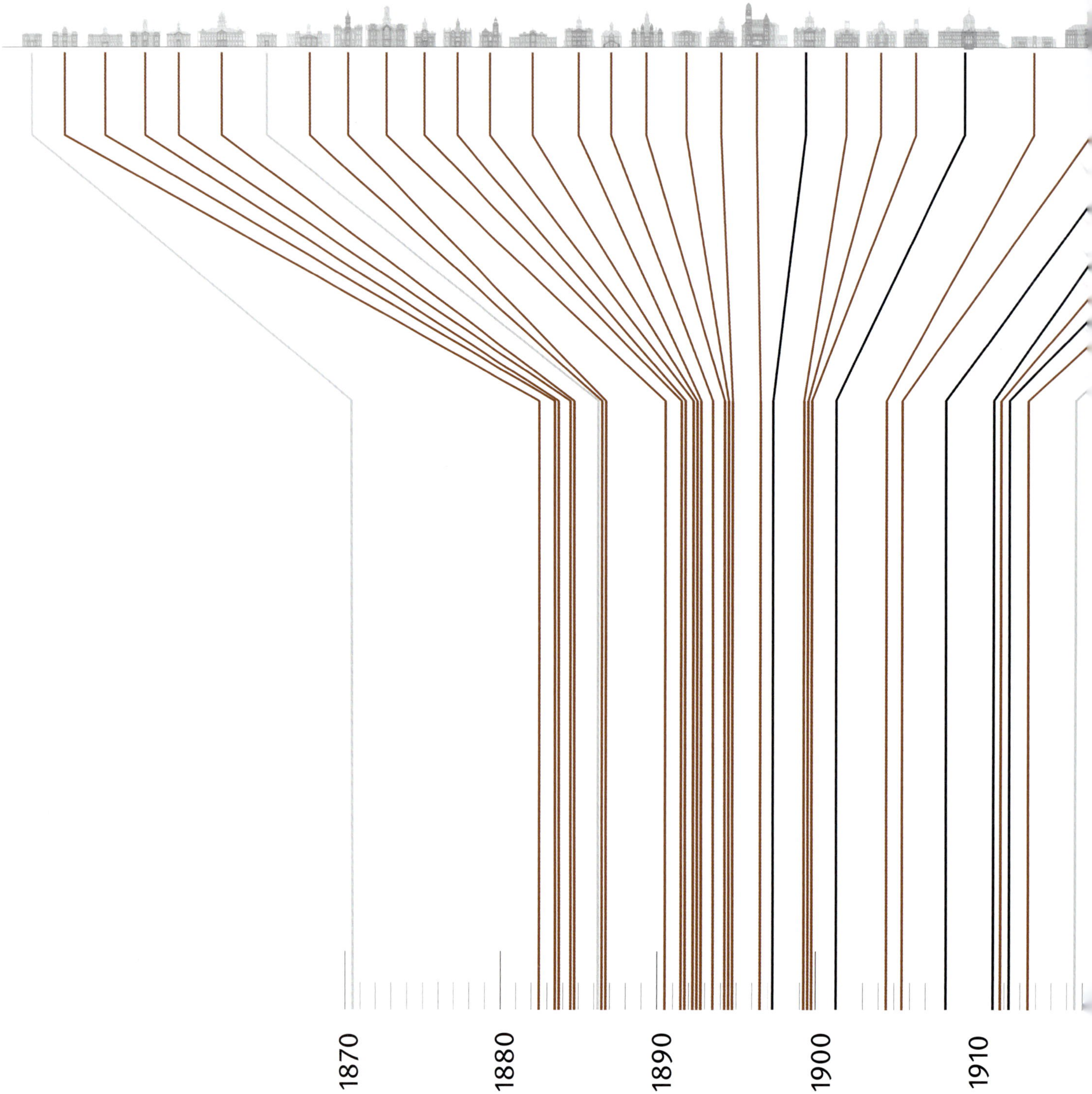
1870
1880
1890
1900
1910

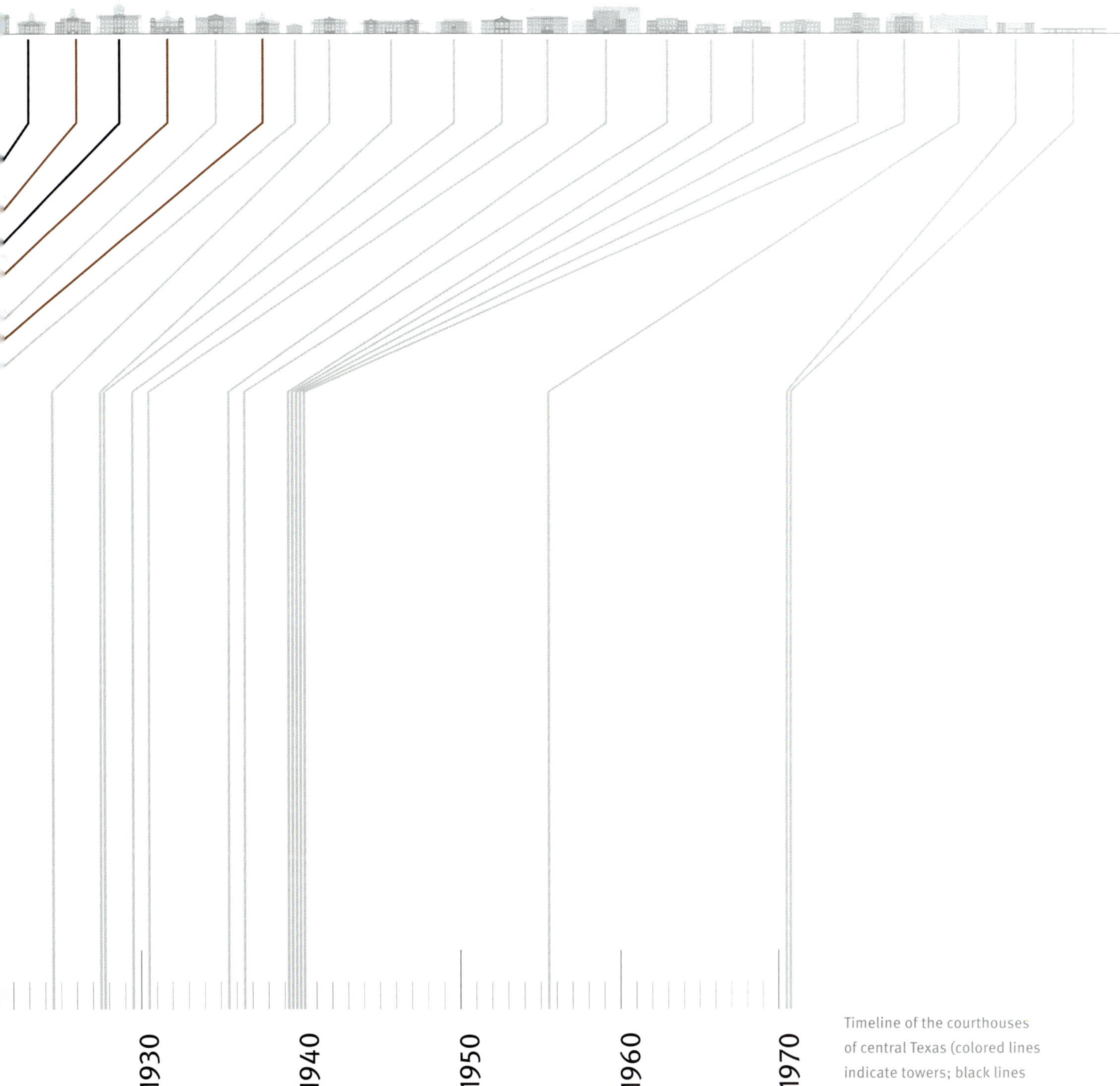

Timeline of the courthouses of central Texas (colored lines indicate towers; black lines indicate domes)

displacement ventilation system, or stack effect, varied from one courthouse to another, but in some cases enough air could be moved to effectively cool courtroom and office spaces to between seventy-eight and seventy-nine degrees Fahrenheit during the hottest days of August.[17] Before the era of air conditioning, this represented a significant relief from the oppressive Texas summer.

Although a range of vertical articulation strategies were used by courthouse architects in central Texas, their actual deployment was concentrated. Beginning in the 1880s, a two-decade era of tower construction was followed by a shorter period of dome construction. No towers or domes were built in central Texas after 1916. Changing stylistic desires and an increased use of mechanical air conditioning systems rendered these architectural elements unnecessary.

In addition to eliminating the towers and domes that had been popular in the previous decades, courthouses built in the teens lacked the articulated massing and vertical emphasis of earlier designs. This new generation of courthouses reflected the declining relative importance of county government as the state began to urbanize at a more rapid pace.[18] The 1920s saw a continuation of this trend. Courthouses increasingly became simple rectangular masses with portico elements added to frame main entrances. Compositions became more horizontal and ornament became less intricate, with a greater differentiation between front and side façades. These entrances typically led to the same crossing corridor layout seen in earlier courthouse designs.

The architectural restraint of the 1920s foreshadowed the abstraction of the modernistic courthouses built in the 1930s. These structures, often executed with the support of Depression-era federal assistance programs such as the Public Works Administration, stripped away traditional massing and ornamentation and replaced it with abstracted geometric forms and patterns. Unlike other strains of modernism that explicitly advanced a social agenda, Depression-era modernism in Texas harbored no progressive ambitions. The desire was instead for the *appearance* of modernity.[19]

Rather than departures from the designs that preceded them, Depression-era courthouses can be understood as attempts to create an architecture that acknowledged contemporary economic, construction, and aesthetic realities while attempting to remain a part of a larger historical continuum. Traditional ornament was abstracted and modernized but not eliminated. Familiar materials such as granite and limestone were not rejected but were finished in a more contemporary way using new technologies. The architectural goal was still to create a courthouse with a monumental public presence even if this was achieved through alternate means.

Typically rectangular in plan, Depression-era courthouses exhibited a hierarchical differentiation between the major and minor façades. Although early examples retained the crossing corridor plan of earlier designs, this was eventually eliminated in place of a single formal entry.[20]

By 1950, the number of people living in the cities of Texas surpassed its rural population for the first time.[21] Counties and the rural parts of the state they governed were no longer the center of economic and political power of the state. With the changing relevance of county government, architectural tastes changed as well. The functional determinism of the modern movement was embraced completely, and courthouses no longer sought to maintain any aesthetic connection to earlier architectural precedents. Rationalizing the construction of opulent courthouse designs became all the more problematic as the cost of building materials and labor continued to increase. As a result of these issues and in response to an ever-growing need for administrative space, courthouses began to resemble office buildings in both function and form. Only their placement on a central square provided these midcentury modern courthouses with public presence.[22]

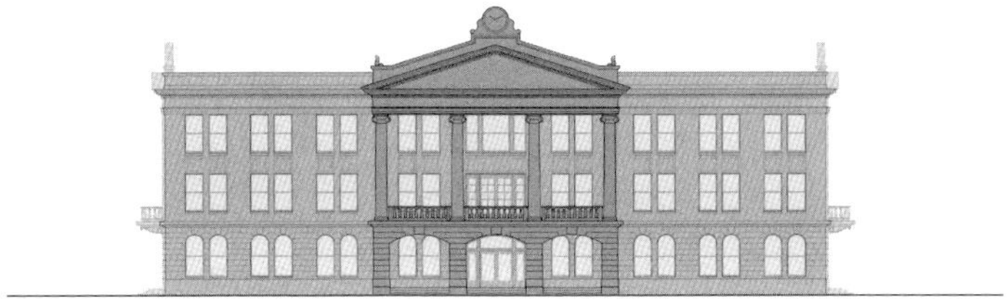

Uvalde County Courthouse, 1927, Uvalde, Texas

Gillespie County Courthouse, 1939, Fredericksburg, Texas

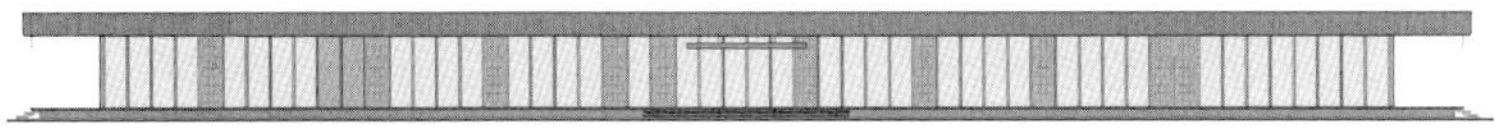

Zavala County Courthouse, 1970, Crystal City, Texas

The Courthouses of Central Texas

From the eclectic detailing of the courthouse in Atascosa County to the austere horizontality of the courthouse in Zavala County, the courthouses of central Texas represent a varied collection of formal and stylistic approaches. When studied as a group, subtle commonalities and evolving trends quickly become visible.

If the elevation profiles of each of these courthouse buildings are overlaid on top of one another, the dominating towers of the Bexar, Hill, and Navarro courthouses exist as barely perceptible formal outliers, while a much more familiar figure emerges at the diagram's center. Modest in scale and with a tall central tower, this implied form could be said to represent an "average" courthouse silhouette. The emergence of this figure is curious given that less than half of the courthouses in central Texas share anything resembling that particular profile. Just as many are flat-roofed affairs with neither dome nor tower. More specific overlay groupings reveal that while the range of diversity is wide when considering all fifty courthouses, those of particular eras show more consistency with one another.

In the pages that follow, a mix of historical and contemporary data is provided for each county courthouse studied. This includes the year the county was established by the Texas Legislature, its current population according to the 2010 United States census data, the year the studied courthouse was completed, and any significant alteration that occurred that was not undone by a subsequent restoration. A list of existing similar courthouse designs is also provided for reference.

When examined individually, these buildings represent a diverse assortment of forms and styles that speak to both the time of their construction and the affluence of the constituencies that built them. Each tells a compelling story, and each merits individual study.

The courthouses of central Texas, profile overlay, 1870–1970

Courthouse profile overlay, 1870–1899

Courthouse profile overlay, 1900–1916

Courthouse profile overlay, 1917–1929

Courthouse profile overlay, 1930–1970

1870 Kendall County

BOERNE, TEXAS

COUNTY ESTABLISHED: 1862
2010 POPULATION: 33,410

1870: built, Philip Zoeller and S. F. Stendeback
1886, 1910: significant additions
2010: restored (THCPP), Wagner and Klein

SIMILAR TO: Kinney

In addition to being the only county in Texas established during the Civil War, Kendall County also contains the second oldest courthouse in the state. (The Cass County Courthouse, located in far east Texas, antedates the Civil War.) Since the original limestone structure has been added to incrementally, it is possible to read the growth of the county indexed by the changing styles of subsequent additions. The courthouse began with the county's first permanent structure in 1870, a second floor was added in 1886, and a new Italianate façade was added by Alfred Giles in 1910. The majority of county offices were relocated to a new facility across the street from the original building in 1998.

Note: for elevation drawings, 1 inch equals approximately 18 feet. For site plan drawings, north aligns with the top of the page and 1 inch equals approximately 222 feet.

1882 Robertson County

FRANKLIN, TEXAS

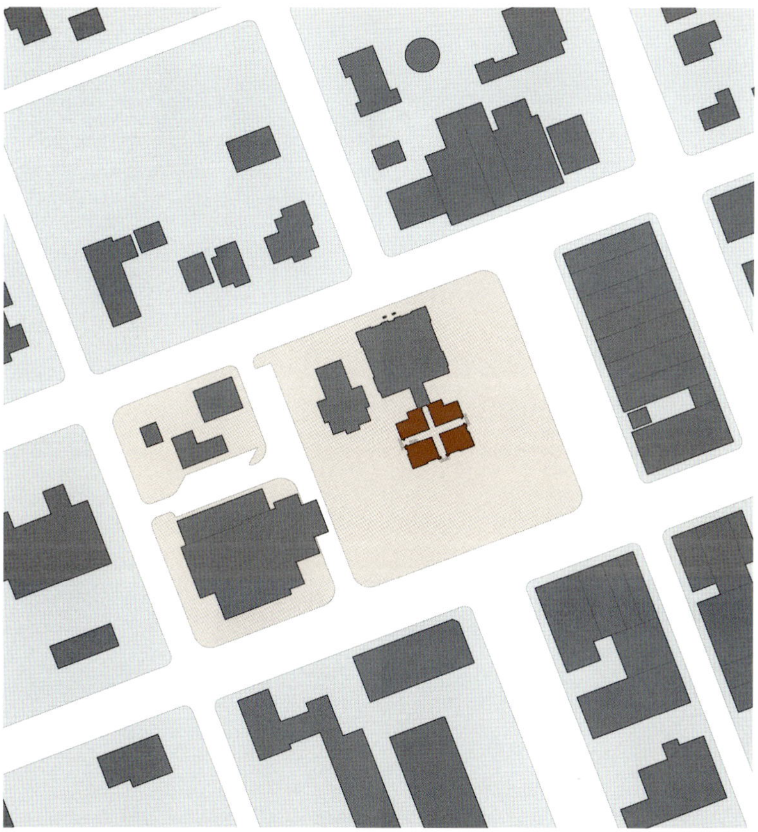

COUNTY ESTABLISHED: 1837
2010 POPULATION: 16,622

1882: built, F. E. Ruffini
2014: restored (THCPP), Sinclair and Wright Architects[1]

SIMILAR TO: Ozona

A 1924 remodeling altered the roofline of the Robertson County Courthouse and gave the limestone structure concrete entry porticos and superficial mission-style details. These alterations were removed during the restoration, completed in 2014, that returned the courthouse to its original appearance with mansard roofs at each corner pavilion and a short tower marking the center entrance.

The courthouse sits on a square offset relative to the rest of Franklin's street grid. This allows the courthouse to sit prominently at the end of Center Street. Two small blocks are created as a result of this shift, one of which has been taken over by the sheriff's department.

1883 Bastrop County

BASTROP, TEXAS

COUNTY ESTABLISHED: 1836
2010 POPULATION: 74,141

1883: built, J. N. Preston / F. E. Ruffini
1923: skinned in plaster, tower reduced

SIMILAR TO: Blanco

The feel of the Bastrop County Courthouse changed significantly when stucco was applied over the brick exterior of what had been a courthouse with fine Italianate detailing. Cornice and entry portico details were also removed in an attempt to modernize the building. The net result is that the rich texture of the original 1880s building is lost. This is especially apparent given the fact that the neighboring jail retains its original detailing and exposed brickwork. The effect is a curious one. The courthouse looks like a contemporary attempted re-creation of a historical courthouse rather than a highly modified original.

Although other courthouses had their towers removed completely, in Bastrop the tower merely had its upper twenty feet removed and the lower portion encased in copper. The resulting tower appears undersized relative to the rest of the courthouse.

1883

Lampasas County

LAMPASAS, TEXAS

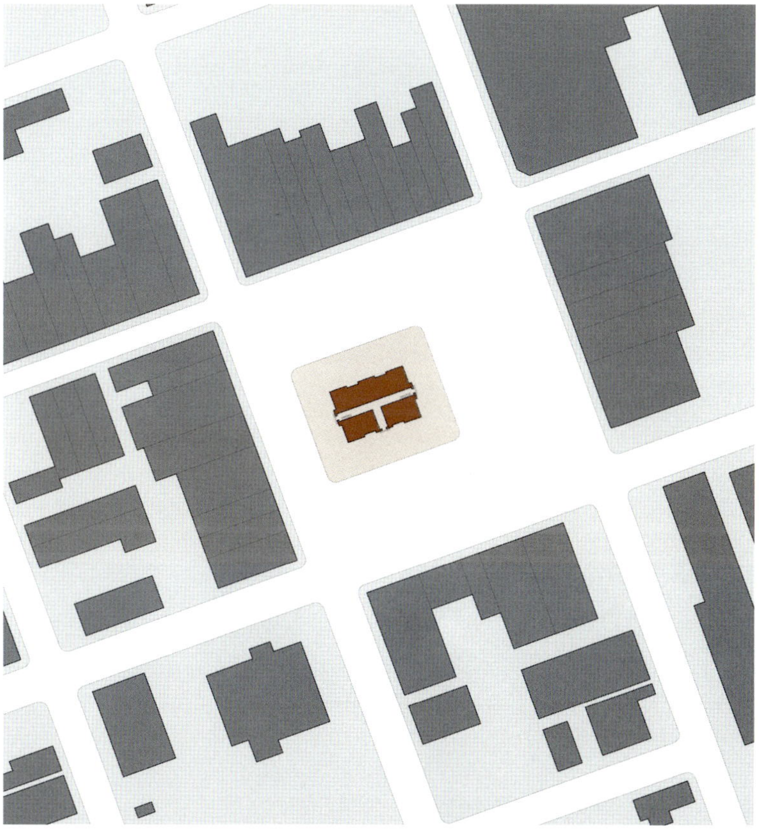

COUNTY ESTABLISHED: 1856
2010 POPULATION: 19,677

1883: built, W. C. Dodson
2004: restored (THCPP), Komatsu Architecture

SIMILAR TO: Hill, Hood, Parker

While Dodson created a number of formally similar courthouses throughout his career, the building in Lampasas was one of the first to be comprised of a base topped by mansard roofs and an ornate central tower. The Hill County Courthouse represents one of the larger, more ornate versions of Dodson's standard courthouse design, whereas the Lampasas courthouse is considerably smaller than his later designs, with only two rather than three floors. The resulting composition is more horizontal than Dodson's other projects.

In many ways, the Lampasas County Courthouse represents a transition between the first-generation courthouses and the more ornate structures that would be built in the closing decades of the nineteenth century. The simple massing of its limestone base exists in contrast to the intricate detailing of its roofline and tower.

1884

Wilson County

FLORESVILLE, TEXAS

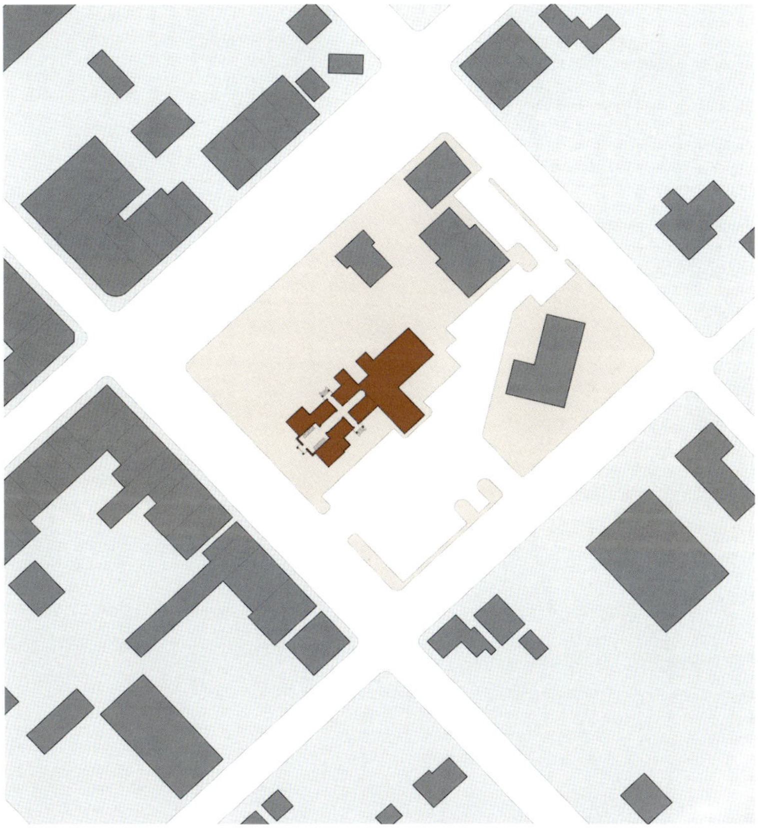

COUNTY ESTABLISHED: 1860
2010 POPULATION: 42,918

1884: built, Alfred Giles
1936: skinned in plaster

SIMILAR TO: Grimes

The Italianate Wilson County Courthouse is one of the few in the state that possesses a significant interior entry lobby. Located underneath the main tower, the two-story space contains a grand stair leading to the second-floor district courtroom, while a single main corridor accesses the first-floor offices. The building originally possessed a brick exterior but was encased in stucco in the mid-1930s.

Though several annexes have been built on the courthouse square over the years, the presence of the courthouse remains strong, especially its main southwesterly façade. The courthouse is also the oldest one still in use in the state that was built to an original Alfred Giles design.[2]

1884

Bell County

BELTON, TEXAS

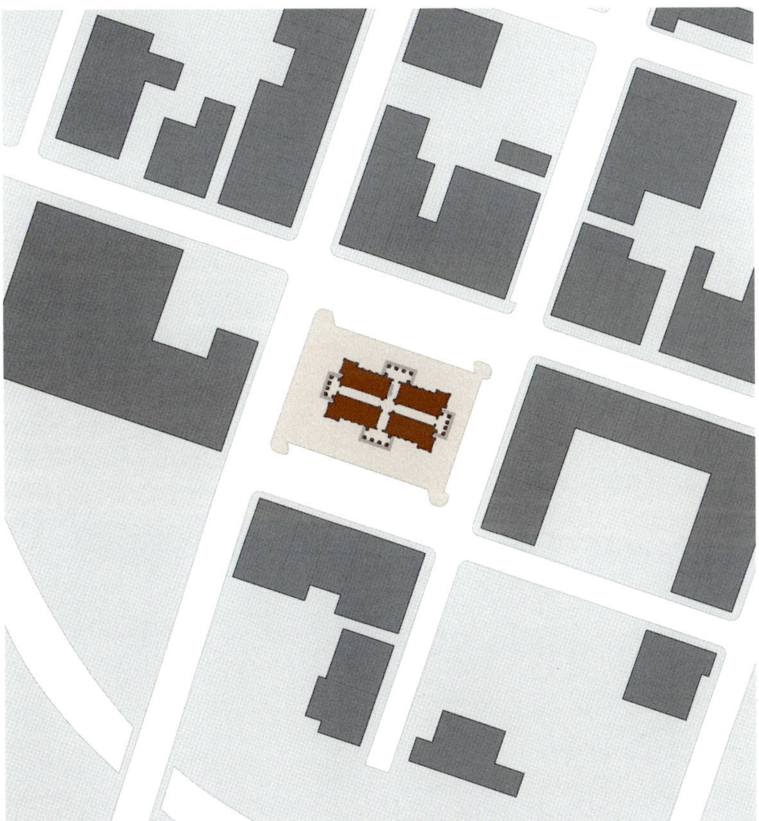

COUNTY ESTABLISHED: 1850
2010 POPULATION: 310,235

1884: built, J. N. Preston and Son
1999: partially restored, TWC Architects

SIMILAR TO: McLennan

Each façade of Bell County's sizable Renaissance Revival limestone courthouse is endowed with a colonnaded portico reminiscent of the Capitol buildings in Washington, DC, and Austin. Like its marble and granite counterparts, the courthouse has its dome rendered in lighter metal as opposed to stone to save cost and ease constructability. Unlike its formal relatives, this "dome" is square in plan.[3]

The county's courthouse square is nestled into a bend of a tributary of the Leon River. Although the courthouse was once surrounded on all four sides by commercial buildings, its western block has since been replaced by a sizable sheriff's office and jail complex.

1886 Leon County

CENTERVILLE, TEXAS

COUNTY ESTABLISHED: 1846
2010 POPULATION: 16,801

1886: built, William Johnson
2007: restored (THCPP), Sinclair and Wright Architects

SIMILAR TO: McMullen

Although more ornate courthouses were being constructed in the 1880s, the brick cube in Centerville provides an example of a transitional structure that straddled the divide between later first-generation courthouses and early Victorian structures. The Leon County Courthouse differs from the standard first-generation prototype in that it never had a cupola and has but a single hallway on its lower level as opposed to the typical set of crossing corridors.

The dimensions of the 1886 courthouse were the same as those of the county's previous 1856 courthouse because county officials decided to reuse the existing foundations in order to reduce construction costs.

1886 Hamilton County

HAMILTON, TEXAS

COUNTY ESTABLISHED: 1856
2010 POPULATION: 8,517

1886: built, E. D. Williams (superintendent)[4]
1931: wings added / tower removed
2012: restored (THCPP), Komatsu Architecture

SIMILAR TO: none

One of the most idiosyncratic courthouses in the state, the Hamilton County Courthouse represents an extreme amalgamation of historical styles. Built of limestone in the Second Empire style in 1886, its tower and mansard roofs were removed in a 1931 remodeling that saw the addition of two large wings and entry porticos. These modifications changed the emphasis of the composition from vertical to horizontal. The added crenellated towers gave the courthouse a medieval flavor, while the oddly proportioned portico was classical in design. A small tower of uncertain stylistic origin was added to replace the much larger one that had been removed in the 1930s. This smaller tower was itself removed shortly after its initial construction, and its reconstruction proved highly controversial during the courthouse's recent restoration. It was rebuilt even though few images documented, and even fewer residents could recall, its curious appearance.

1886

Bosque County

MERIDIAN, TEXAS

COUNTY ESTABLISHED: 1854
2010 POPULATION: 18,212

1886: built, J. J. Kane
2007: restored (THCPP), ARCHITEXAS

SIMILAR TO: Shackelford

The limestone Bosque County Courthouse existed in its original condition for fifty years before a significant remodeling in the 1930s removed its Gothic-inspired roof and towers in an attempt to give the building a more contemporary appearance. It remained in this altered state for seventy years before an equally significant restoration effort returned it to its original configuration.[5]

In addition to its physical transformation, another feature that makes the courthouse unique is the two “front” entrances that flank its main tower. This element is not centered as it is in many other courthouses but rather is offset to the northeast side of the structure.

1890 Hill County

HILLSBORO, TEXAS

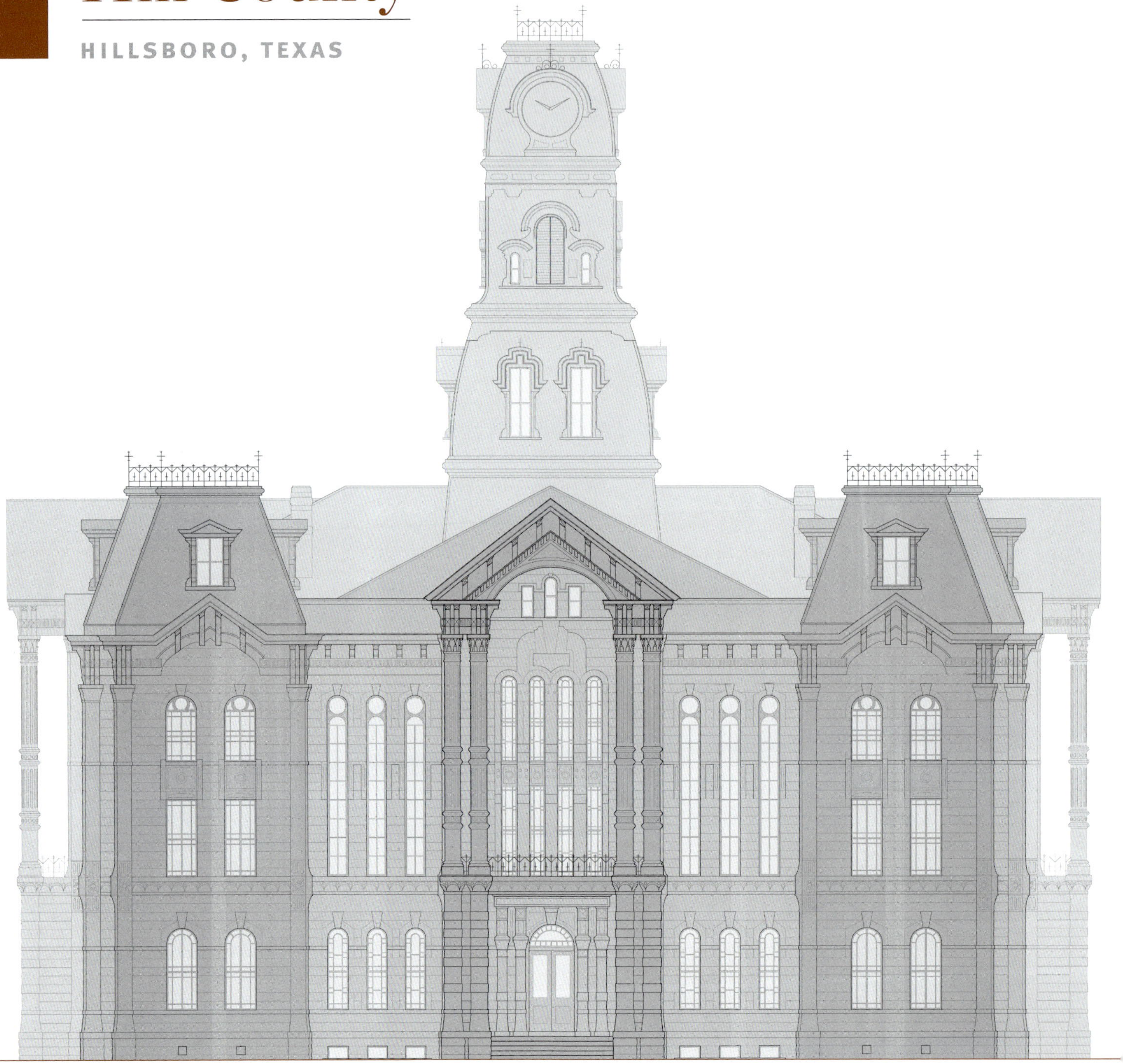

COUNTY ESTABLISHED: 1853
2010 POPULATION: 35,089

1890: built, W. C. Dodson
1999: restored, ARCHITEXAS

SIMILAR TO: Hood, Lampasas, Parker

The Hill County Courthouse represents Dodson's ultimate realization of his vision of courthouse design. With its massive limestone base and soaring Second Empire–style tower, the Hill County Courthouse dominates the flat north-central Texas landscape for miles around. The mostly white palette of materials dramatically reflects the low morning and evening sun.

A fire in 1993 effectively destroyed the building, but an extensive restoration project rebuilt it. This painstaking reconstruction helped inspire the creation of the Texas Historic Courthouse Preservation Program in 1999, which provided both technical and financial resources so that other counties throughout the state could engage in similarly ambitious preservation efforts.

1891 Bandera County

BANDERA, TEXAS

COUNTY ESTABLISHED: 1856
2010 POPULATION: 20,485

1891: built, Benjamin F. Trester / The McDonald Brothers
2007: partially restored (THCPP), Wagner and Klein Architects and Preservation Consultants

SIMILAR TO: Grimes

Located atop a rise of land overlooking the Medina River, the tower of the Renaissance Revival Bandera County Courthouse dominates the town of the same name. Although the tower possesses a clock face on each of its four sides, the hands are painted appliqué. Originally these "fake" hands were set to 7:45. After the tower was restored in 2006, the time was reset to the more aesthetically standard 10:10.

Although "B. F. Trester" is listed as the architect, the courthouse closely resembles those designed by the McDonald Brothers in Kentucky. It appears as if Trester purchased the design from the McDonald Brothers and built several versions of it in Texas after moving there from Indiana.

1891

Fayette County

LA GRANGE, TEXAS

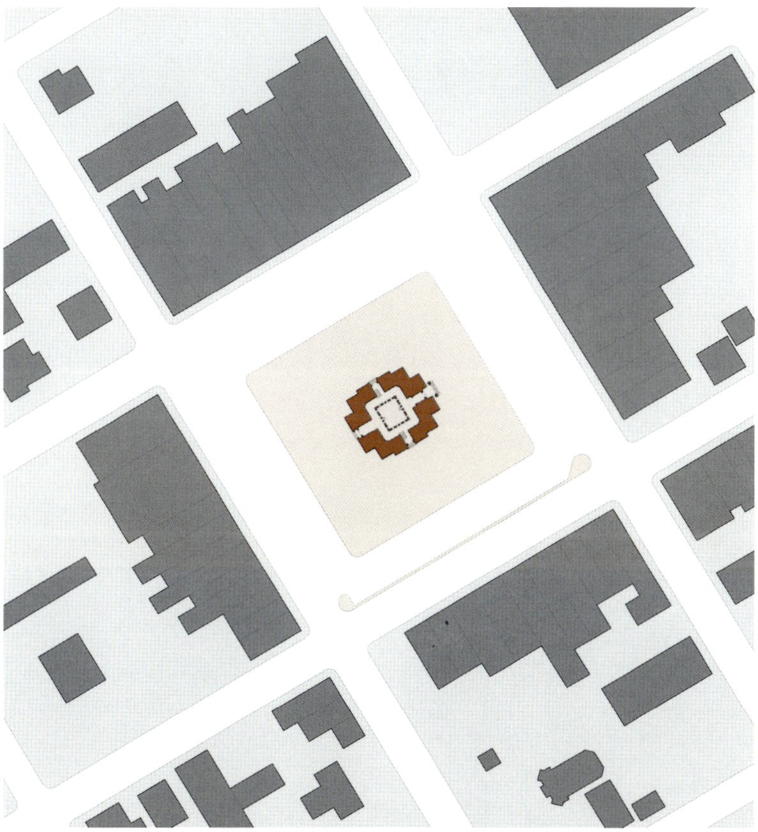

COUNTY ESTABLISHED: 1837
2010 POPULATION: 24,554

1891: built, J. Riely Gordon
2005: restored (THCPP), Volz and Associates

SIMILAR TO: Victoria

The limestone Fayette County Courthouse is organized around what was originally an open central courtyard. Although a glazed skylight has since enclosed this space, the original design allowed both natural ventilation and light to permeate the building. The existence of this internal void required pushing the tower out of its more typical central position, resulting in the increased prominence of one elevation over the others.

Over the years, a few counties in Texas chose to build precinct courthouses to better serve their dispersed populations. Fayetteville's Precinct 2 courthouse exists as an excellent example of a wood frame, first-generation courthouse design.

1892

Llano County

LLANO, TEXAS

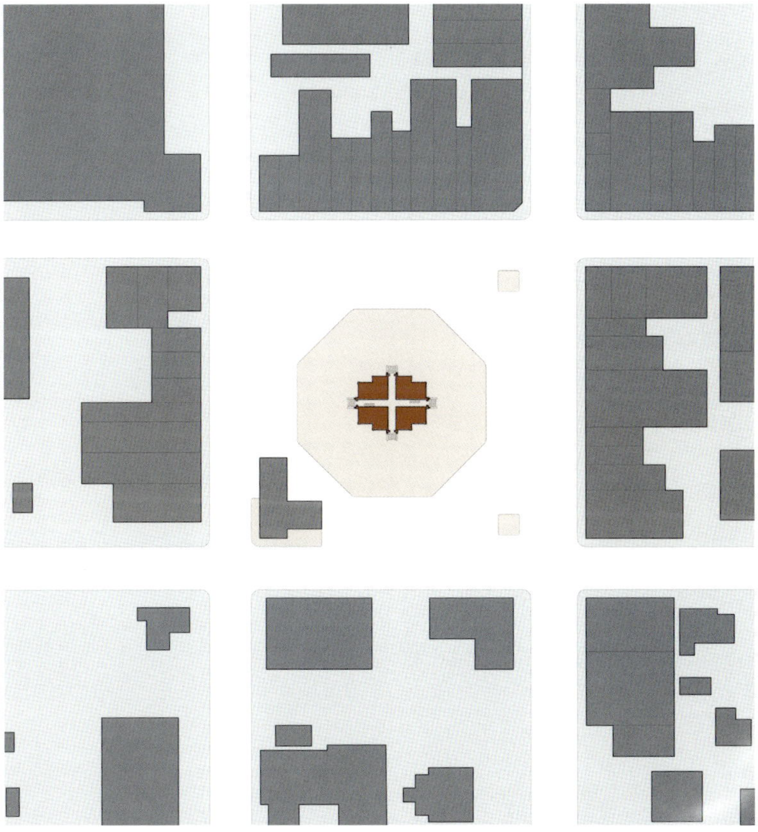

COUNTY ESTABLISHED: 1856
2010 POPULATION: 19,301

1892: built, Larmour and Watson[6]
2002: restored (THCPP), Volz and Associates

SIMILAR TO: none

The formal massing of the Italianate Llano County Courthouse is diagrammatically simple, with four corner pavilions. Three of these are topped by low pyramidal roof structures, while a taller and more ornate tower sits upon the fourth, giving the courthouse its distinctively dynamic appearance. Whereas most courthouse designs embrace symmetry at all costs, in Llano the asymmetry is celebrated.

Although the courthouse square is itself symmetrical, the offset tower makes a gesture toward the nearby Llano River, which flows a few blocks north of downtown. The tower itself has changed appearance several times before finally being restored to its original appearance in 2002. The four-faced clock was not part of the courthouse when it was completed in 1893. As was also the case in other counties, the additional cost of the clock mechanism could not initially be afforded.

1892 Medina County

HONDO, TEXAS

COUNTY ESTABLISHED: 1848
2010 POPULATION: 46,006

1892: built, Martin, Byrnes and Johnston
1942: wings added / tower removed

SIMILAR TO: Throckmorton

The remarkably horizontal, wall-like proportions of the Medina County Courthouse result from significant alterations that were made to the structure in the early 1940s, when the original tower was removed and a set of two-story wings were added to the eastern and western façades.[7] Both wings closely match the limestone detailing of the original Italianate building.

In 2009 the county was awarded a grant to develop the drawings necessary to restore the courthouse to its 1893 appearance. This would have seen the reconstruction of the tower and the removal of the 1942 wings. Responding to voter pressure, the commissioners court voted to reject the grant funds. Thus the courthouse will remain in its current configuration.

1892

Milam County

CAMERON, TEXAS

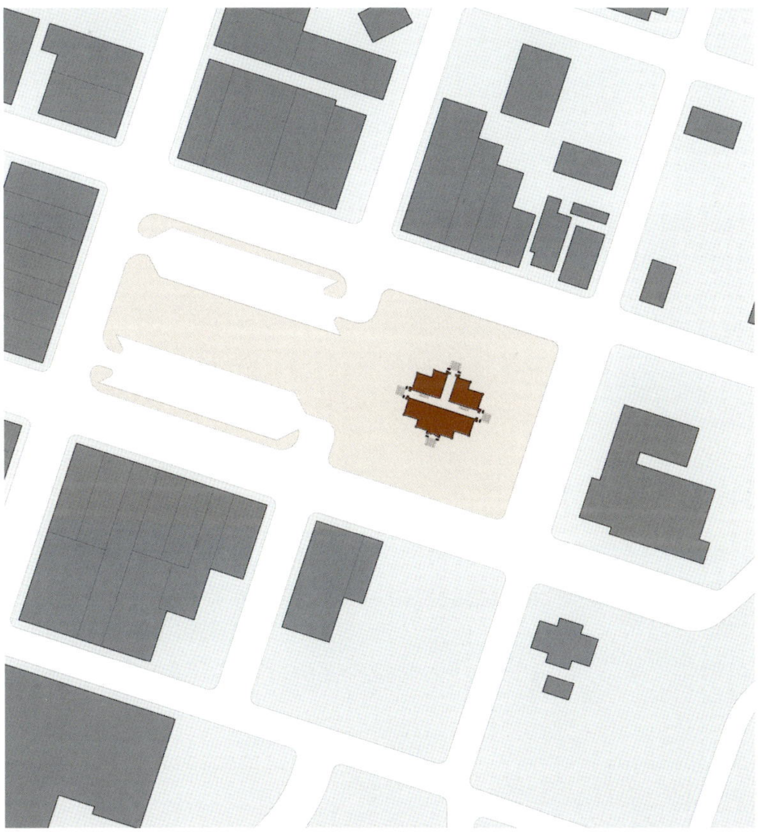

COUNTY ESTABLISHED: 1836
2010 POPULATION: 24,757

1892: built, Larmour and Watson
1998: partially restored, TWC Architects
2002: restored (THCPP), TWC Architects

SIMILAR TO: none

Although not as large as the similarly styled courthouse in Bell County, the Milam County Courthouse includes just as much articulated detail in a much smaller package. With its rusticated limestone base, stacked Corinthian columns and varied pediments, the courthouse represented a refined interpretation of the Renaissance Revival style.[8] For years after a 1938 modernization, the courthouse lacked its signature tower. This was reconstructed when the courthouse was partially restored in 1998.

Although the square to the west of the courthouse has been partially converted to parking, a central strip of landscape and ample perimeter trees still preserve the park-like nature of the space.

1893 Grimes County

ANDERSON, TEXAS

COUNTY ESTABLISHED: 1846
2010 POPULATION: 26,604

1893: built, Glover and Co.
1910: exterior stair added
2002: restored (THCPP), Volz and Associates

SIMILAR TO: Somervell

The Italianate Grimes County Courthouse sits on a prominent rise of land in the smallest county seat in central Texas. Despite the town's small population, its layout is quite developed, with the courthouse square located at the terminus of the town's main commercial street. Because of its location on a promontory, the courthouse dominates both the commercial center of town and the landscape that surrounds it.

Glover made use of portions of the county's previous courthouse, which was destroyed by fire in 1890. In order to provide an alternate means of accessing the second-floor courtroom, a monumental exterior staircase was added to the building in 1910. This significantly altered the overall appearance of the courthouse.

1894 Caldwell County

LOCKHART, TEXAS

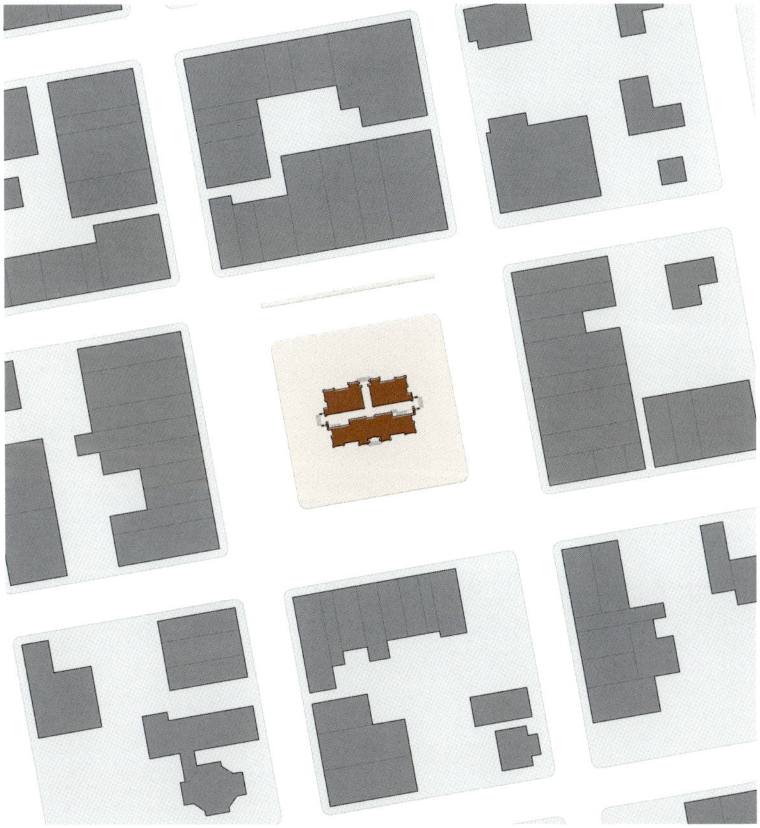

COUNTY ESTABLISHED: 1848
2010 POPULATION: 38,066

1894: built, Henry E. M. Guidon[9]
2000: restored, Volz & Associates / Ford, Powell & Carson

SIMILAR TO: Goliad

Dominating the town of Lockhart, this picturesque assembly of towers sits at the heart of a quintessential courthouse square. Surrounded on all four sides by two- and three-story commercial buildings, the square remains quite lively to this day.

With its rich polychrome stonework and ornate crown of towers, cupolas, and chimneys, the Caldwell County Courthouse's profile changes depending on the viewer's position in town. This tower acts as a landmark and is visible from a distance of several miles outside of town. Though rendered in different materials, the courthouse in Caldwell is nearly identical to the one in Goliad.[10]

1894 Karnes County

KARNES CITY, TEXAS

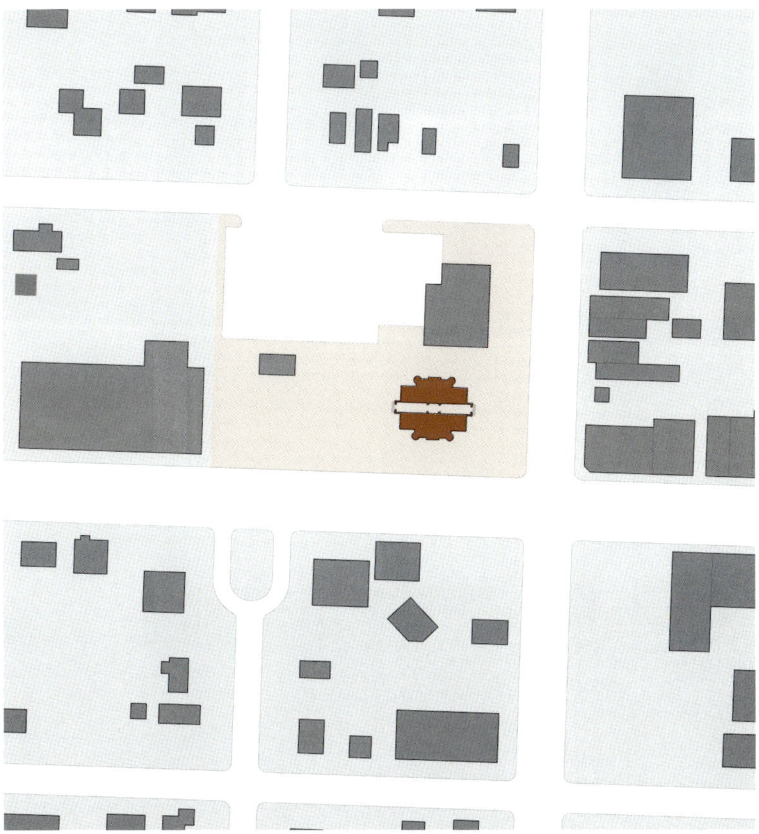

COUNTY ESTABLISHED: 1854
2010 POPULATION: 14,824

1894: built, John Cormack
1924: roofline altered / tower removed

SIMILAR TO: none

The Karnes County Courthouse has suffered from a number of alterations that compromised the original Romanesque design. The building's central tower and various other roof elements were removed, and the building's brick was covered with stucco. As is the case with other "decapitated" courthouses, the resulting composition appears artificially terminated at the roof cornice. A full restoration is currently underway.[11]

A large square consisting of two conjoined city blocks was designated as the site for the courthouse. The current courthouse was built on the southeast corner of this square, leaving the remaining space occupied by various other county facilities.[12]

1894

Gonzales County

GONZALES, TEXAS

COUNTY ESTABLISHED: 1836
2010 POPULATION: 19,807

1894: built, J. Riely Gordon
1997/2000: partially restored, Volz and Associates

SIMILAR TO: Hopkins

One of the many stipulations accompanying both Spanish and Mexican land grants was that settlements had to be laid out according to a set of formal rules. Arranged in a cruciform pattern, three of the five blocks originally designated as public space still exist as open squares in central Gonzales. The county courthouse occupies the center block, which had originally been intended to be the town's public plaza. The Mexican model (like the Spanish model before it) was to place public buildings so that they faced public squares. The American approach was to place public buildings directly on the public squares. Thus Gonzales can be understood as a Hispanic plan developed in a distinctly American manner.

The courthouse is one of Gordon's early cruciform designs, and although the proportions of the brick courthouse are not as elegant as they would become in later designs, the organization of the plan shows considerable skill.

1896

Bexar County

SAN ANTONIO, TEXAS

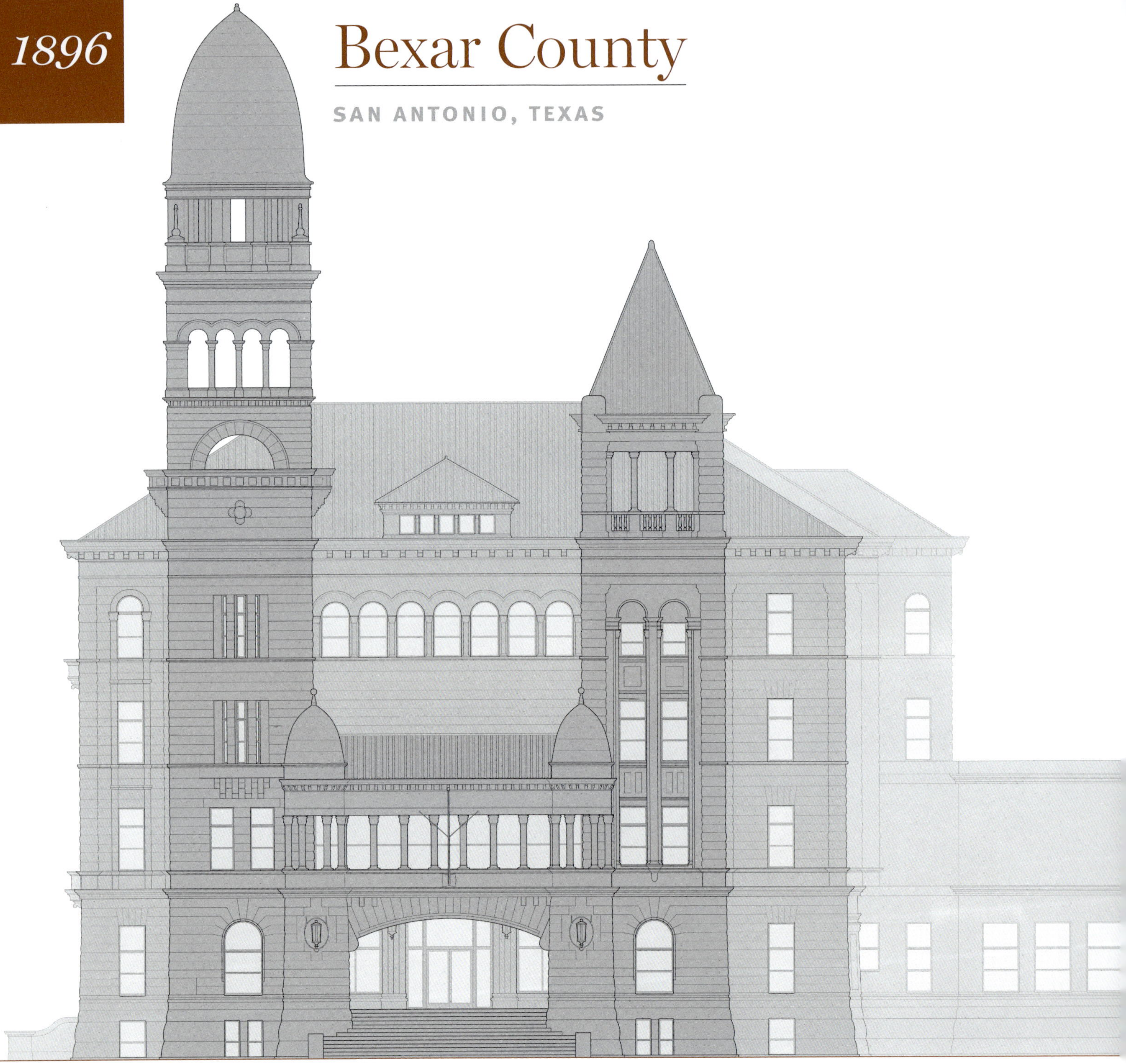

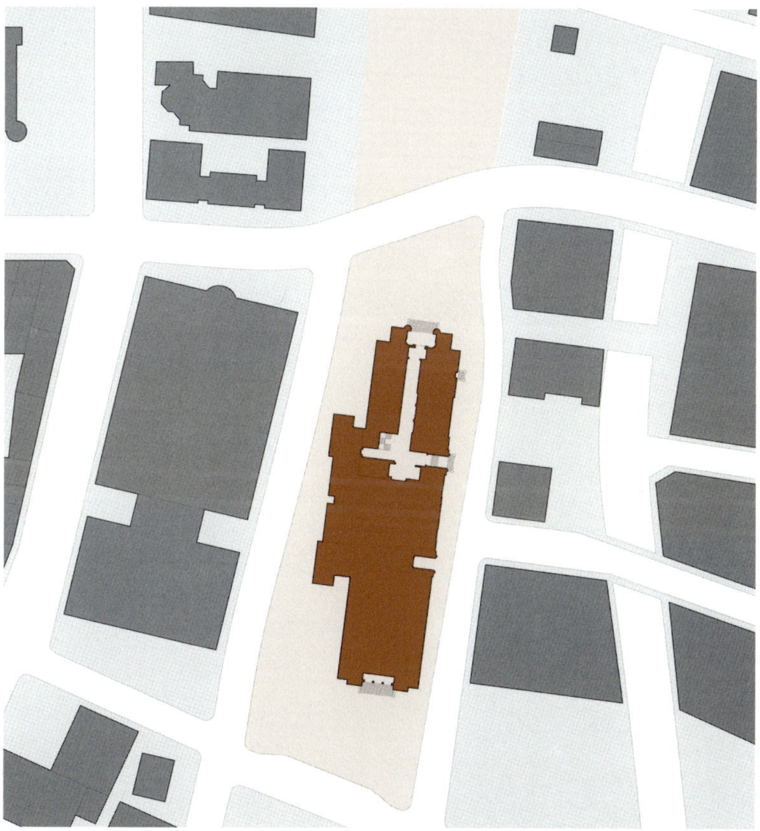

COUNTY ESTABLISHED: 1836
2010 POPULATION: 1,714,773

1896: built, Gordon and Laub
1914, 1927, 1963, 1972: significant additions
2003: partially restored, 3D/International[13]

SIMILAR TO: none

Although it was one of the first courthouses designed by J. Riely Gordon, due to cost overruns and a contentious relationship with the builder, the Bexar County Courthouse was not finished until after several of his other designs had been completed. Unlike most Texas courthouses that sit in isolation on a square, the San Antonio courthouse faces a public plaza, giving its north façade considerably greater urban importance. This placement has also allowed the courthouse to be expanded southward without altering its presence on Main Plaza.

Diagrammatically dissimilar from Gordon's later cruciform courthouse designs, the original C-shaped plan opened to prevailing southeasterly breezes, while its asymmetrical towers created a dynamic composition with the form of the neighboring San Fernando Cathedral.

1897 Coryell County

GATESVILLE, TEXAS

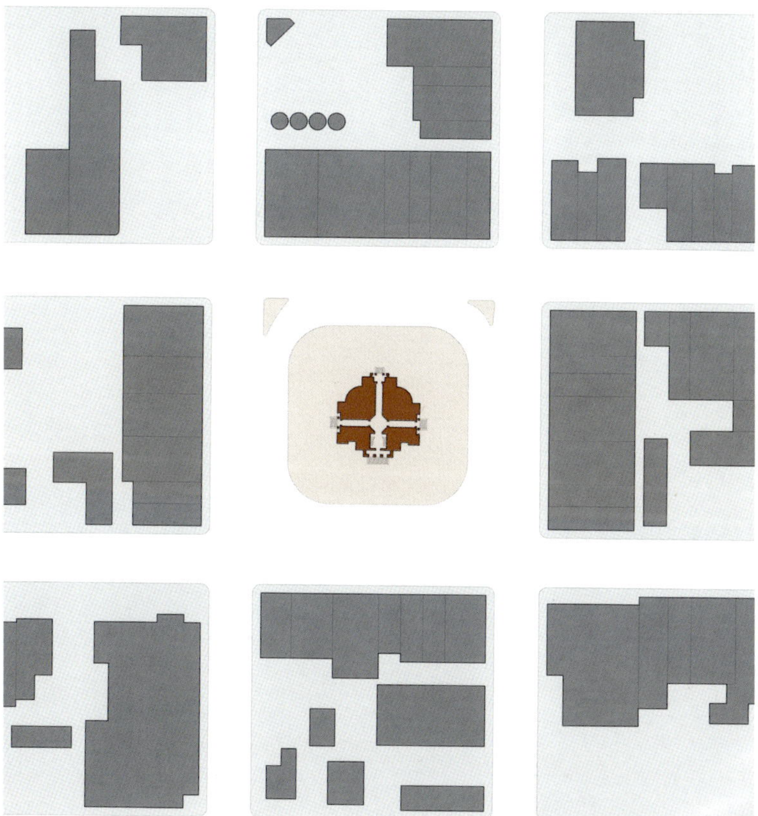

COUNTY ESTABLISHED: 1854
2010 POPULATION: 75,388

1897: built, W. C. Dodson
1987: partially restored, The Williams Company, AIA

SIMILAR TO: Hays

With Second Empire massing, Romanesque detailing, and a Renaissance dome, the Coryell County Courthouse is stylistically eclectic. Dodson appears to have attempted to create a synthesis of the many popular architectural styles in existence at the end of the nineteenth century. This attempt at hybridization can be seen as an effort to update his standard approach to changing architectural tastes.[14] With two bulbous reentrant corners, his project in Coryell County also references the designs of one of his chief architectural competitors, J. Riely Gordon.

Although entrances exist on all four sides of the building, the southern façade receives special emphasis in the form of a monumental colonnade and pediment. As opposed to other courthouses that seek to equalize the importance of all façades, primacy is given to one in Coryell County via a monumental portico.

1898 Comal County

NEW BRAUNFELS, TEXAS

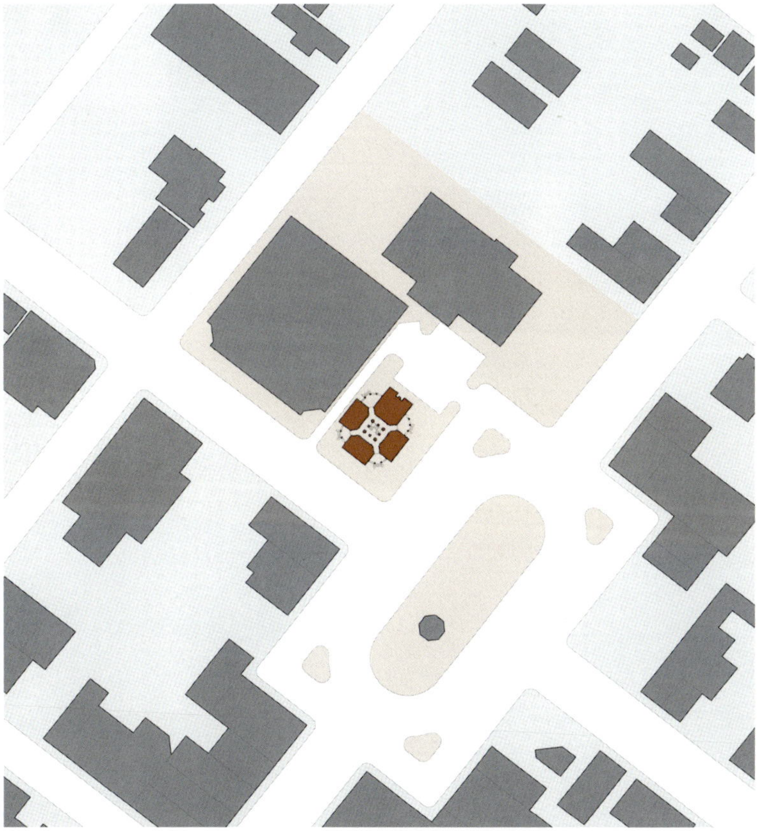

COUNTY ESTABLISHED: 1846
2010 POPULATION: 108,472

1898: built, J. Riely Gordon
2013: restored (THCPP), Volz and Associates

SIMILAR TO: Lee

After increasingly ornate Romanesque courthouse designs, Gordon's limestone courthouse in Comal County was much more restrained than earlier iterations in terms of ornament and color. As such, it reads as an abstracted, streamlined version of his earlier designs. The Comal County Courthouse is nearly identical to the one in Lee County except that the latter is built of brick and has a clock on top of the central tower.[15]

Gordon's cruciform courthouses are ideally suited to their standard location in the center of a courthouse square. In New Braunfels, however, the courthouse sits to one side of the town's main plaza, rendering one of its corner entrances effectively superfluous.

1899 McCulloch County

BRADY, TEXAS

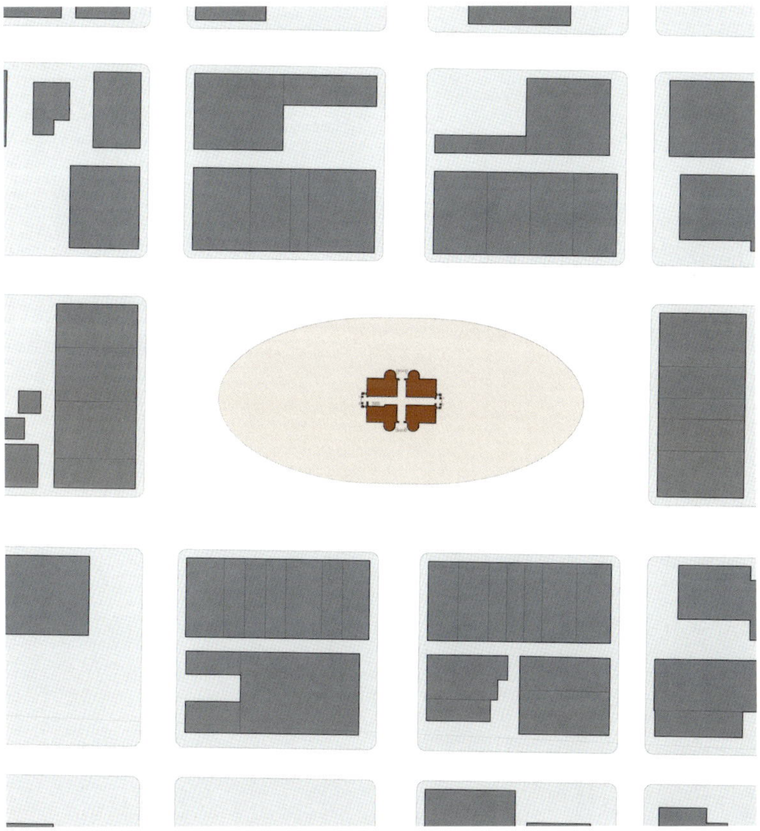

COUNTY ESTABLISHED: 1856
2010 POPULATION: 8,283

1899: built, Martin and Moodie
2009: restored (THCPP), TWC Architects

SIMILAR TO: Throckmorton

Although the Romanesque style had begun to fall out of favor with most architects by the end of the nineteenth century, contractor-led efforts continued to employ the style.[16] The sturdy proportions of the sandstone courthouse in Brady lack the finesse of other Romanesque designs, and the simple renditions of familiar design elements give the building a somewhat abstracted appearance.

As in Mason County, the courthouse in McCulloch County sits in a large square created by the amalgamation of two adjacent city blocks. Its relationship to the surrounding landscape's topography makes the approach to this courthouse especially memorable, with the courthouse sitting upon a pronounced hilltop.

1899 Lee County

GIDDINGS, TEXAS

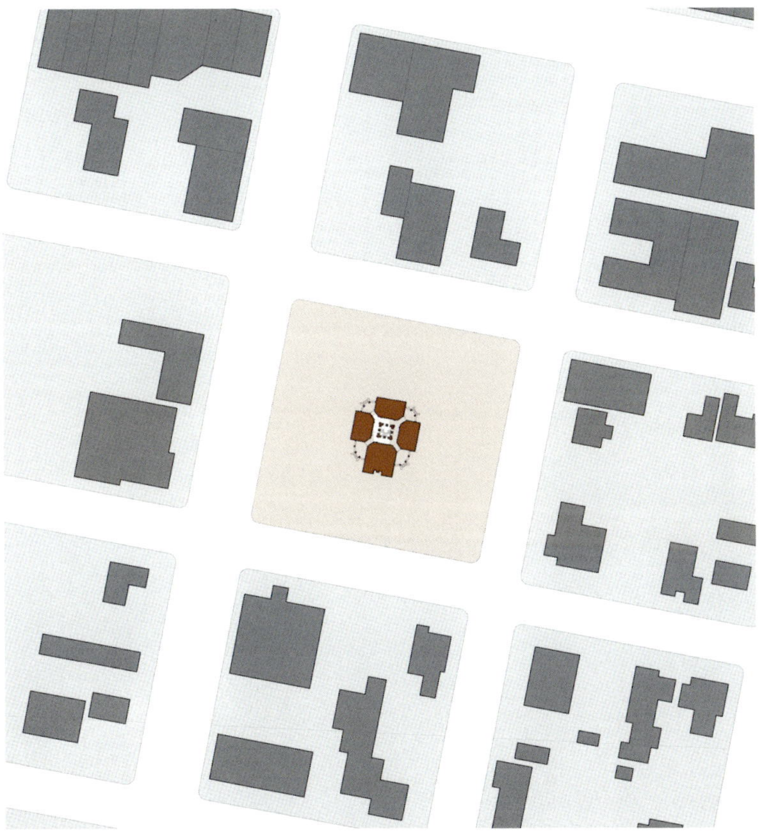

COUNTY ESTABLISHED: 1874
2010 POPULATION: 16,612

1899: built, J. Riely Gordon
2004: restored (THCPP), Architects Rabe + Partners

SIMILAR TO: Comal

Although the Lee County Courthouse was designed and built concurrently with the one in Comal County, the soil upon which it was built in Giddings is much worse than that in New Braunfels. Issues relating to the differential settlement of the building's foundation have plagued the building since it was completed.

When the railroad came through Giddings, it pulled commercial development away from the courthouse square and created a new center around the passenger station. This explains why today the Lee County Courthouse is somewhat isolated from the county seat's main commercial core.

1901

McLennan County

WACO, TEXAS

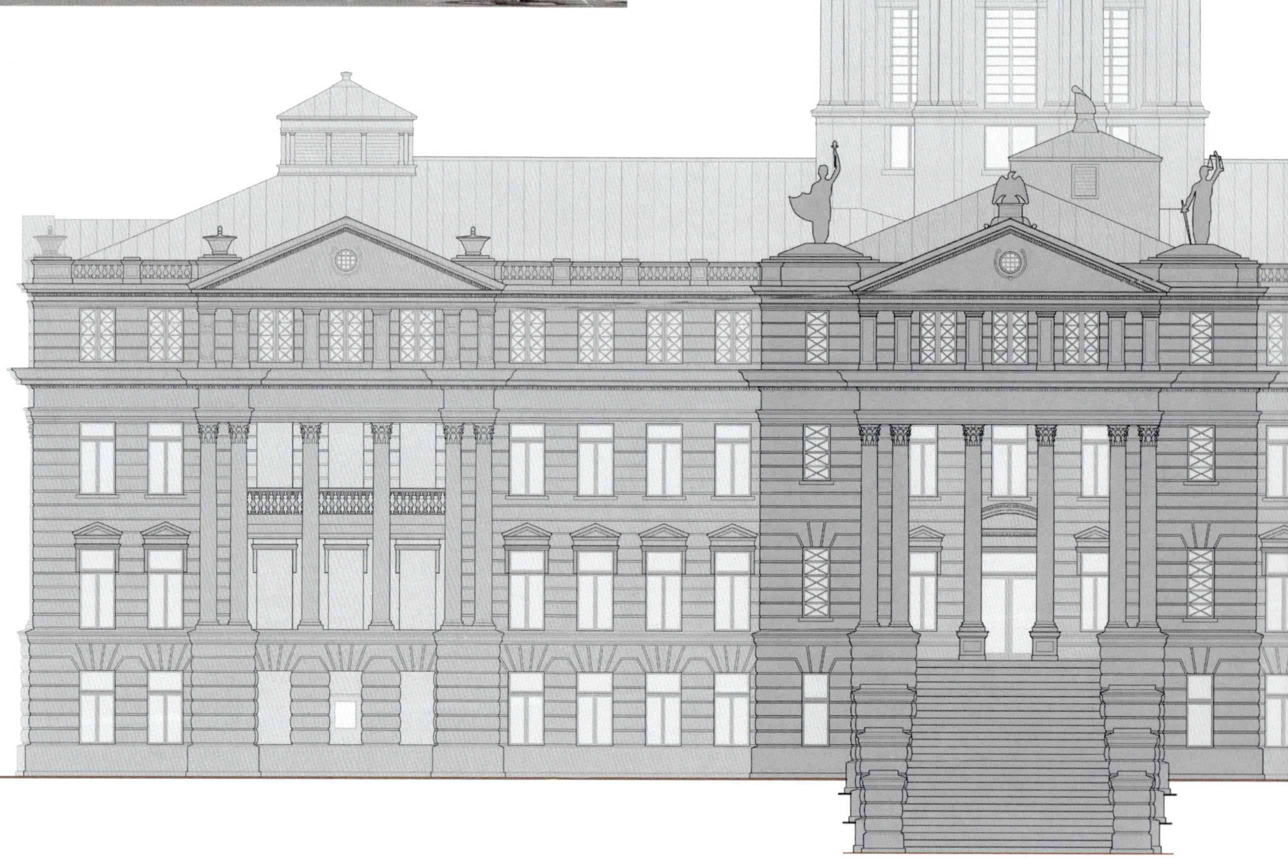

COUNTY ESTABLISHED: 1850
2010 POPULATION: 234,906

1901: built, J. Riely Gordon
2012: partially restored (THCPP), ARCHITEXAS

SIMILAR TO: Bell, Navarro

The limestone McLennan County Courthouse is probably the most architecturally ambitious courthouse in central Texas. With a floor extending above the main entablature and flanking engaged porticos, the massing of the courthouse reflects a Beaux-Arts influence while details remain true to its classical precedents. The dome is a scaled and simplified version of the one sitting atop St. Peter's in Rome. Representing a clear break from his earlier cruciform courthouse designs, this courthouse proved that Gordon could execute multiple architectural styles with great virtuosity and skill.

The courthouse square sits oddly isolated from the rest of downtown Waco. Instead of facing a commercial block or plaza, the grand façade of the McLennan County Courthouse today faces a paved surface parking lot.

1904

Frio County

PEARSALL, TEXAS

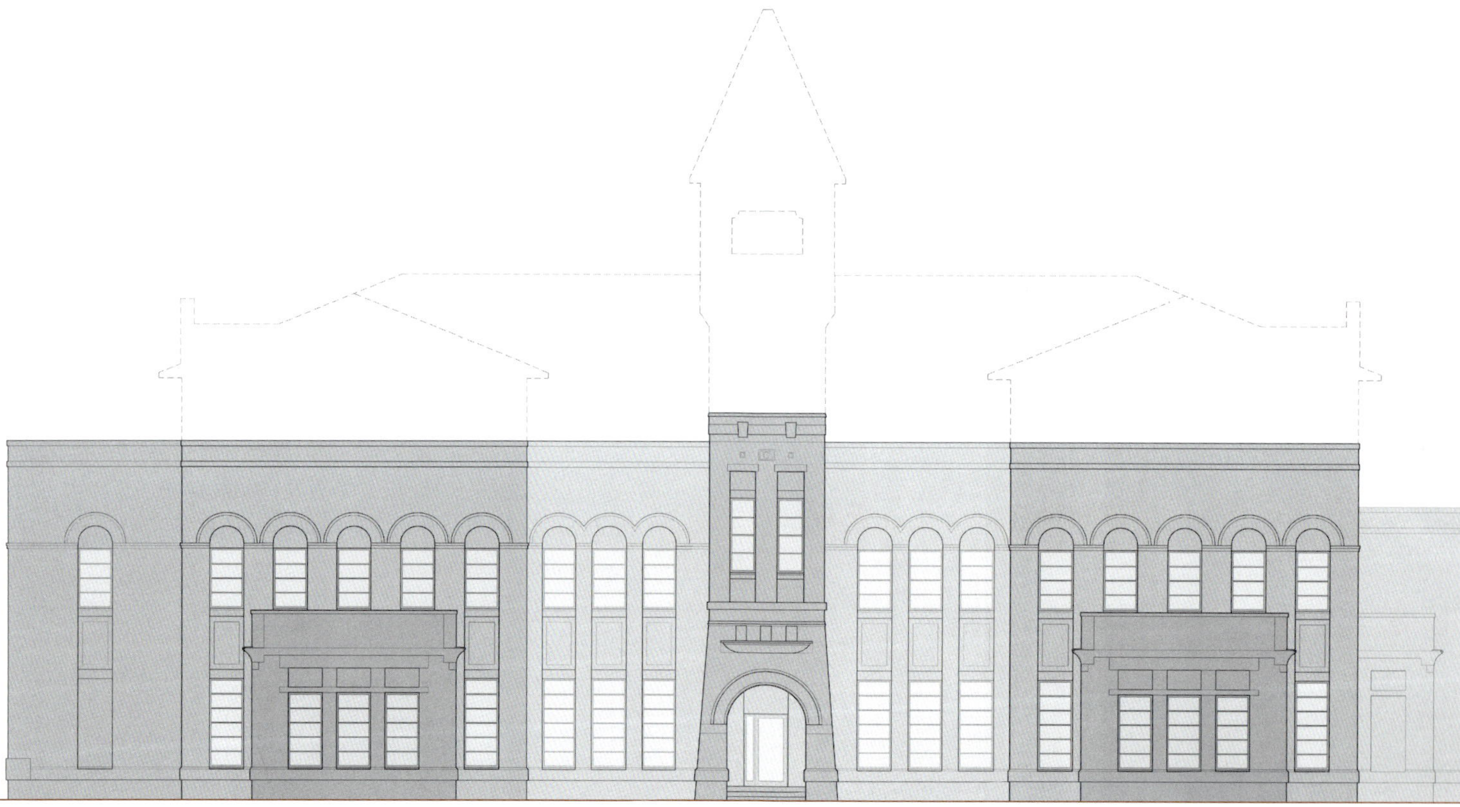

COUNTY ESTABLISHED: 1871

2010 POPULATION: 17,217

1904: built, Henry T. Phelps

1938: third story / tower removed

SIMILAR TO: Runnels

One of the results of the preservation efforts in the state of Texas is that the unrestored courthouse is now a noteworthy exception. Although the current state of the Frio County Courthouse is compromised, that condition is not new.

When originally constructed, the brick Romanesque courthouse had three stories and a tower marking the main entry. In 1938 that tower was removed along with the structure's entire third story. Although one explanation for the removal of the tower points to a severe bat infestation, this does little to suggest why the third story was removed, especially since an addition of a nearly identical size was constructed at the same time. A more likely explanation is that the structure was poorly designed or constructed, and the removal was necessitated for safety reasons. Whatever the reason for this alteration, the result is a diminished structure that lacks most of its defining detail. Numerous additions in the decades that followed have created a courthouse with an awkward amalgamation of styles and masses.

1905

Navarro County

CORSICANA, TEXAS

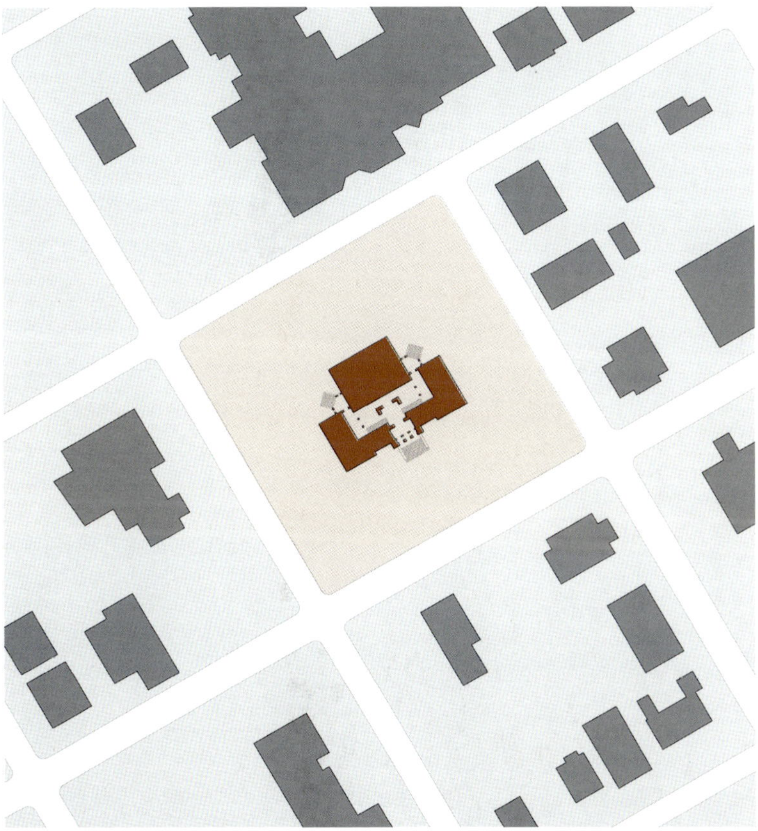

COUNTY ESTABLISHED: 1846
2010 POPULATION: 47,735

1905: built, J. E. Flanders
2013: partially restored (THCPP), 1113 Architects

SIMILAR TO: Cooke

Seen from a distance, the Navarro County Courthouse towers above the surrounding canopy of trees to peer over the town of Corsicana. Located on a hill on the edge of a residential neighborhood, it sits several blocks away from its town's main commercial district.

Although the courthouse demonstrates the Beaux-Arts style in its massing, much of its detailing betrays a Prairie style influence. Sitting atop this building is a unique tower-dome of a girth unlike any other in the state. The square rotunda underneath this tower-dome is likewise a type of space not typically found in a courthouse. All of this makes the Navarro County Courthouse easily recognizable.

1908 Hays County

SAN MARCOS, TEXAS

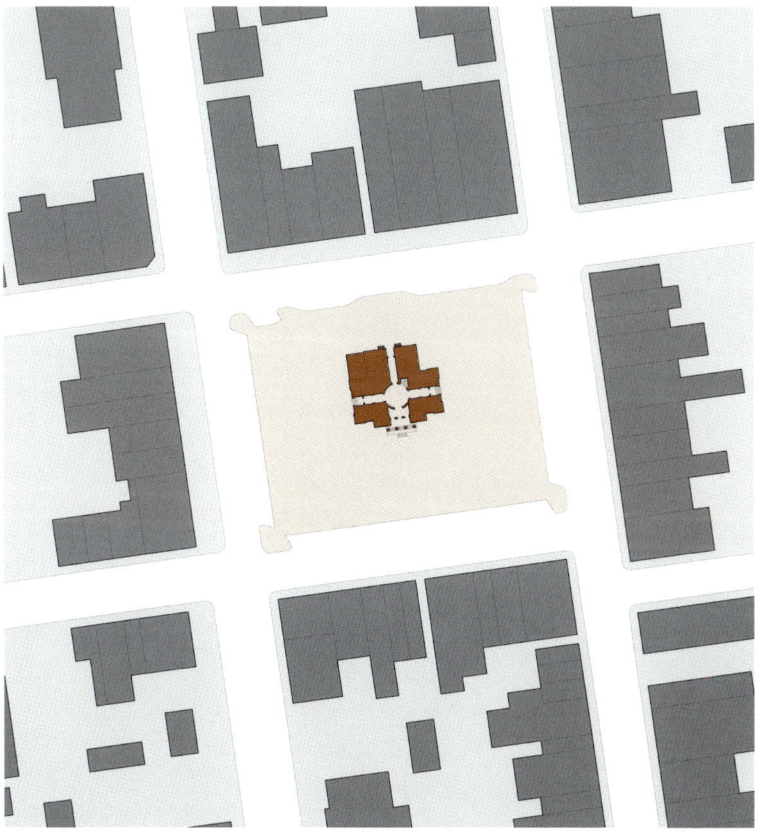

COUNTY ESTABLISHED: 1848
2010 POPULATION: 157,107

1908: built, Charles H. Page and Brother
1998: restored, Ford, Powell and Carson

SIMILAR TO: Bee, Coryell, Fort Bend

The courthouse square of Hays County is unusual in that it slopes noticeably form north to south. This creates a southern elevation that is approximately ten feet higher than the northern, giving the brick courthouse that sits upon it a notably monumental southern façade. The entry portico and side pavilions are proportionally elongated and reinforce the vertical emphasis of the courthouse.

Although the Hays County Courthouse possesses the crossing corridor plan found in most courthouses, the existence of a dome provides the opportunity for an internal rotunda. As a result of the windowless dome, the rotunda is artificially lit. Thus, the Beaux-Arts courthouse possesses a monumental internal space that matches the grand scale of the exterior.

1909 Mason County

MASON, TEXAS

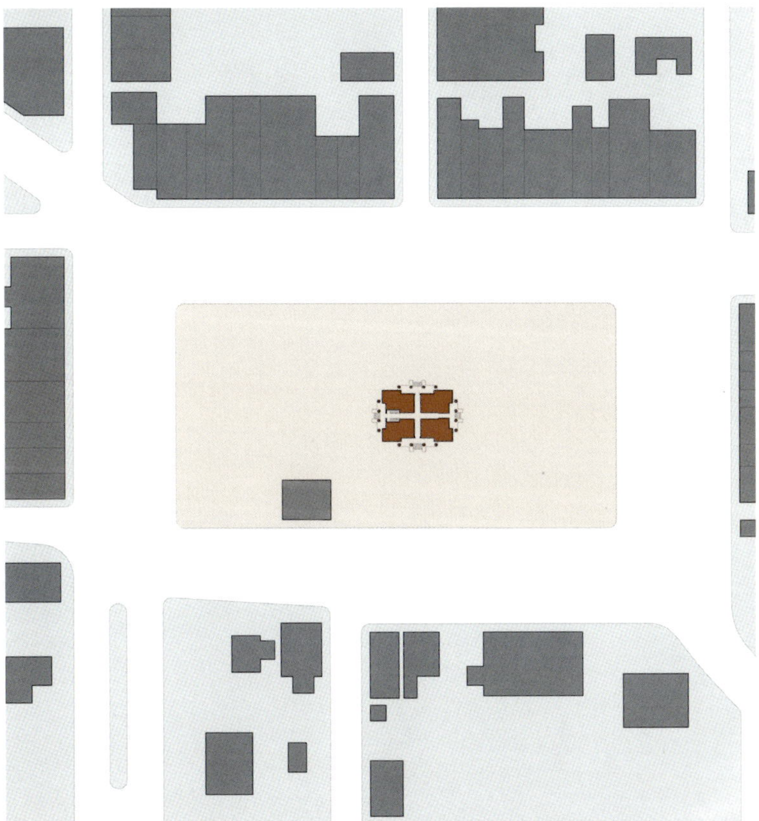

COUNTY ESTABLISHED: 1858
2010 POPULATION: 4,012

1909: built, Edward C. Hosford
2013: partially restored (THCPP), TWC Architects / Lord Aeck Sargent

SIMILAR TO: Franklin, Jeff Davis

With its dome and colonnaded porticos, the classical courthouse in Mason County is a handsome enough structure. What sets it apart, however, is its setting within two conjoined city blocks in the center of town. Unlike most courthouse squares, where the courthouse dominates the landscape that surrounds it, this square dominates the building. The commercial buildings of Mason face this park-like square and provide an additional layer of urban framing.

US Highway 87 approaches the center of Mason at an oblique angle and sets up angled views of the Mason County Courthouse dome that are sometimes visible over the trees of the courthouse square.

1911 San Saba County

SAN SABA, TEXAS

COUNTY ESTABLISHED: 1856
2010 POPULATION: 6,131

1911: built, Walter W. Chamberlin

SIMILAR TO: Eagle Pass, Montague

Architects practicing in the Victorian era enjoyed considerable flexibility when it came to creatively rearranging the details and proportions of established historical styles. Those practicing the Renaissance Revival style were typically restrained by more prescriptive architectural rules, but the San Saba County Courthouse shows that similar play could occur within the more staid Renaissance language.

Although its proportions are at times awkward, and some of the intersecting elements are unresolved, the San Saba County Courthouse is an energetic architectural statement. Rather than importing classicism directly to Texas, this courthouse proposed a way that architects could adapt the style in order to make it more intrinsically Texan.

1911

Williamson County

GEORGETOWN, TEXAS

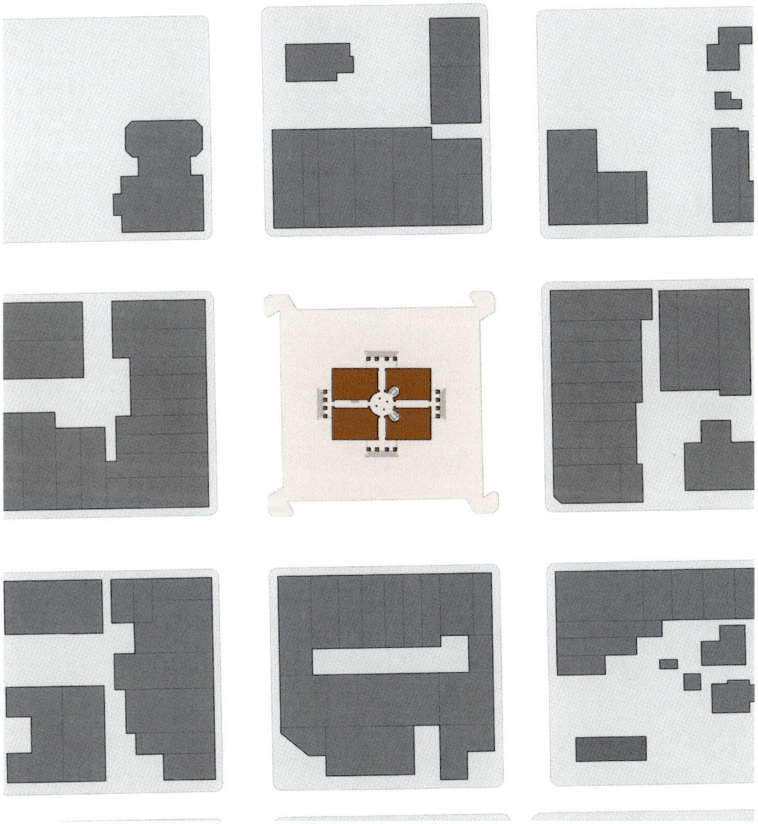

COUNTY ESTABLISHED: 1848
2010 POPULATION: 422,679

1911: built, Charles H. Page
2007: restored (THCPP), 1113 Architects

SIMILAR TO: Anderson

As is the case in Hays County, the Williamson County Courthouse dome house rests upon a drum that does not elevate it sufficiently, so it is mostly obscured when seen from the street. Nevertheless, the proportions of the brick building are handsome, and it sits in the middle of one of the liveliest courthouse squares in central Texas.

Cotton production drove the county's economic growth at the beginning of the twentieth century, and Georgetown's fortuitous location near Austin transformed it into a suburb of that community toward the end of the same century. Even so, the courthouse square still very much reads as an artifact of a century ago.

1912

Atascosa County

JOURDANTON, TEXAS

COUNTY ESTABLISHED: 1856
2010 POPULATION: 44,911

1912: built, Henry T. Phelps, Architect
2003: restored (THCPP), Fisher Heck Architects, Inc.

SIMILAR TO: none

Although several Spanish missions exist throughout the state, the Atascosa County Courthouse is one of the only existent courthouses in Texas to be constructed in a mission-revival style.[17] That said, the dark brick, clay tile roof, and tower elements reference the missions of California rather than those of nearby San Antonio. Because of its curious Sullivanesque detailing, the composition is more eclectic than regional.

The courthouse is also noteworthy in that it is symmetrical about its two main axes and placed within a circular courthouse "square." Architecturally this square is not well defined, with most commercial development occurring along nearby Oak Street.

1913 Mills County

GOLDTHWAITE, TEXAS

COUNTY ESTABLISHED: 1887
2010 POPULATION: 4,936

1913: built, Henry T. Phelps
2011: restored (THCPP), 1113 Architects

SIMILAR TO: Brown, Uvalde, Wood

Like other courthouses of the teens and twenties, the Mills County Courthouse is a brick box with engaged classical porticos articulating three of its four façades. Its strong but quiet presence ensures that the building operates as a background building for its community rather than acting as a focal point, as was the case with courthouses of earlier eras.

Although the structure never contained a dome or tower, a small rotunda penetrates the building's main floors, allowing daylight to enter into the center of the building from a rooftop skylight. Thus the internal benefits of a rooftop element were achieved without the expense of actually constructing one.

1916 Blanco County

JOHNSON CITY, TEXAS

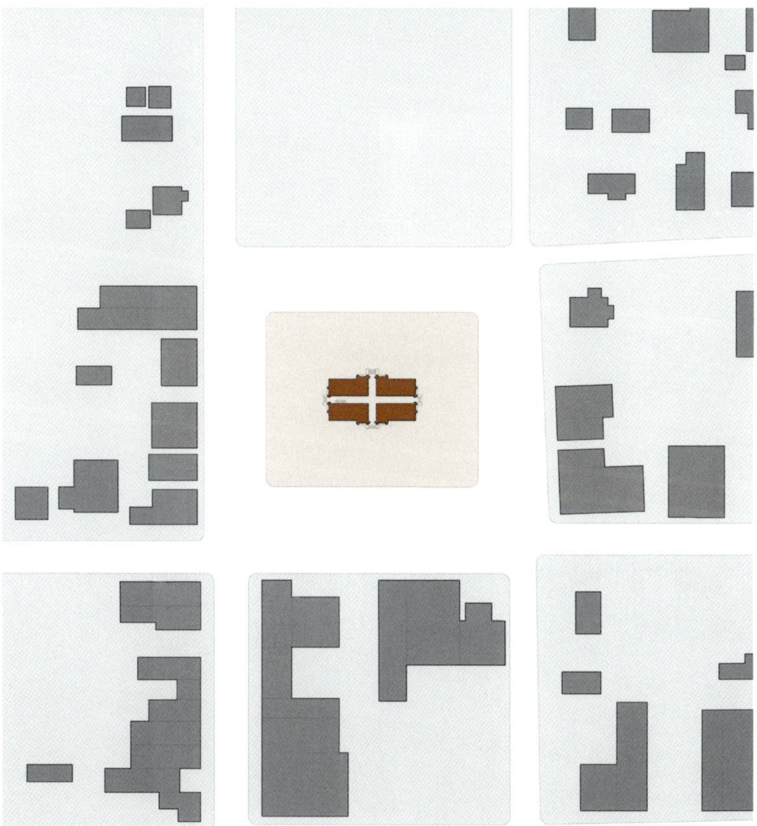

COUNTY ESTABLISHED: 1858
2010 POPULATION: 10,497

1916: built, Henry T. Phelps

SIMILAR TO: Bastrop

The town of Blanco was the seat of Blanco County from its inception until 1890, by which time nearby Johnson City had grown large enough to win an election to move the county seat.[18] This event was highly contested and resulted in a shooting that left one man dead and a sheriff's deputy wounded.

The resulting courthouse sits one block from the main commercial strip of Johnson City. Its four classical porticos do not stand free of the building's main mass but are engaged to it, giving the structure a somewhat flattened feel. The quarry-faced finish of the limestone endows the project with a more rustic appearance.

1917

Real County

LEAKEY, TEXAS

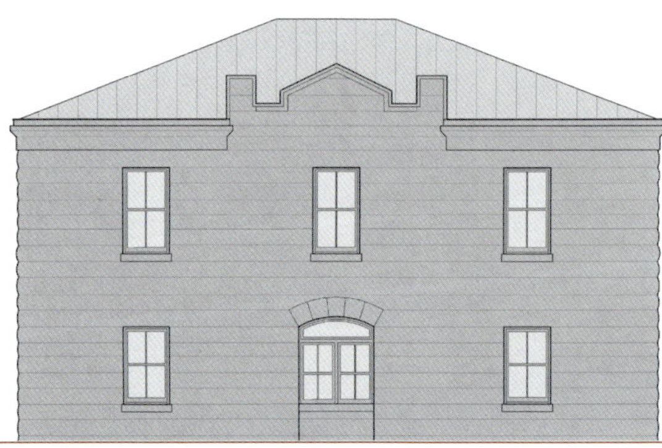

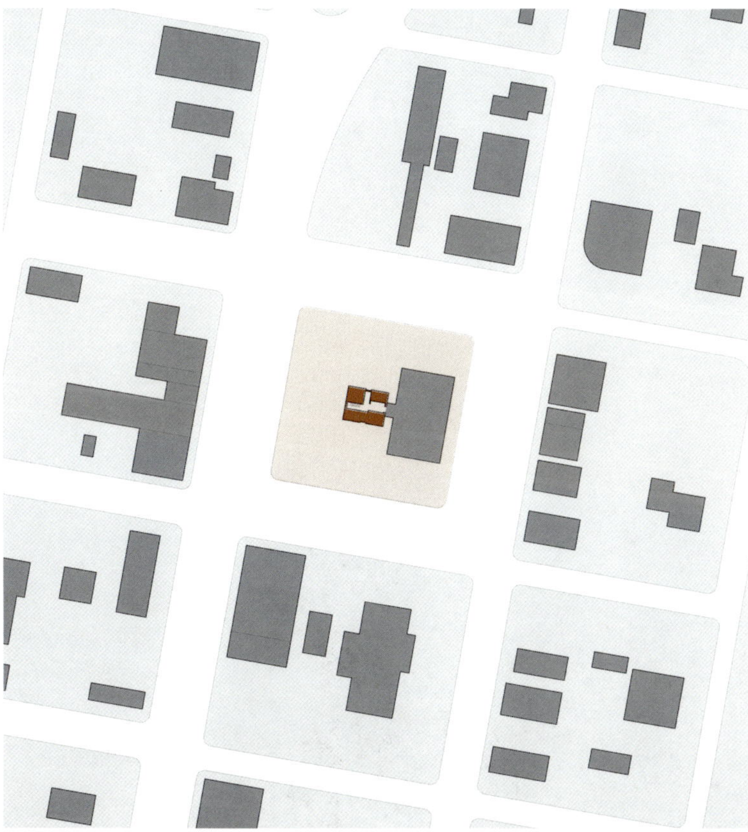

COUNTY ESTABLISHED: 1913
2010 POPULATION: 3,309

1917: built, H. A. Reuter

SIMILAR TO: Edwards, Leon

One of the least populated counties in central Texas, Real County was also the last to be established in the region. The simple stone courthouse in Leakey would be a good example of the type of rugged, first-generation courthouse built in the mid-1800s, were it not built in 1917. Its anachronistic appearance speaks to the austerity of the county and the difficulty of building there, even after the turn of the twentieth century.

A 1978 annex more than doubled the total square footage of the original limestone courthouse. Doors on the original building were converted into windows, and the facility is now entered through the connection between the old and new structures.

1919 Freestone County

FAIRFIELD, TEXAS

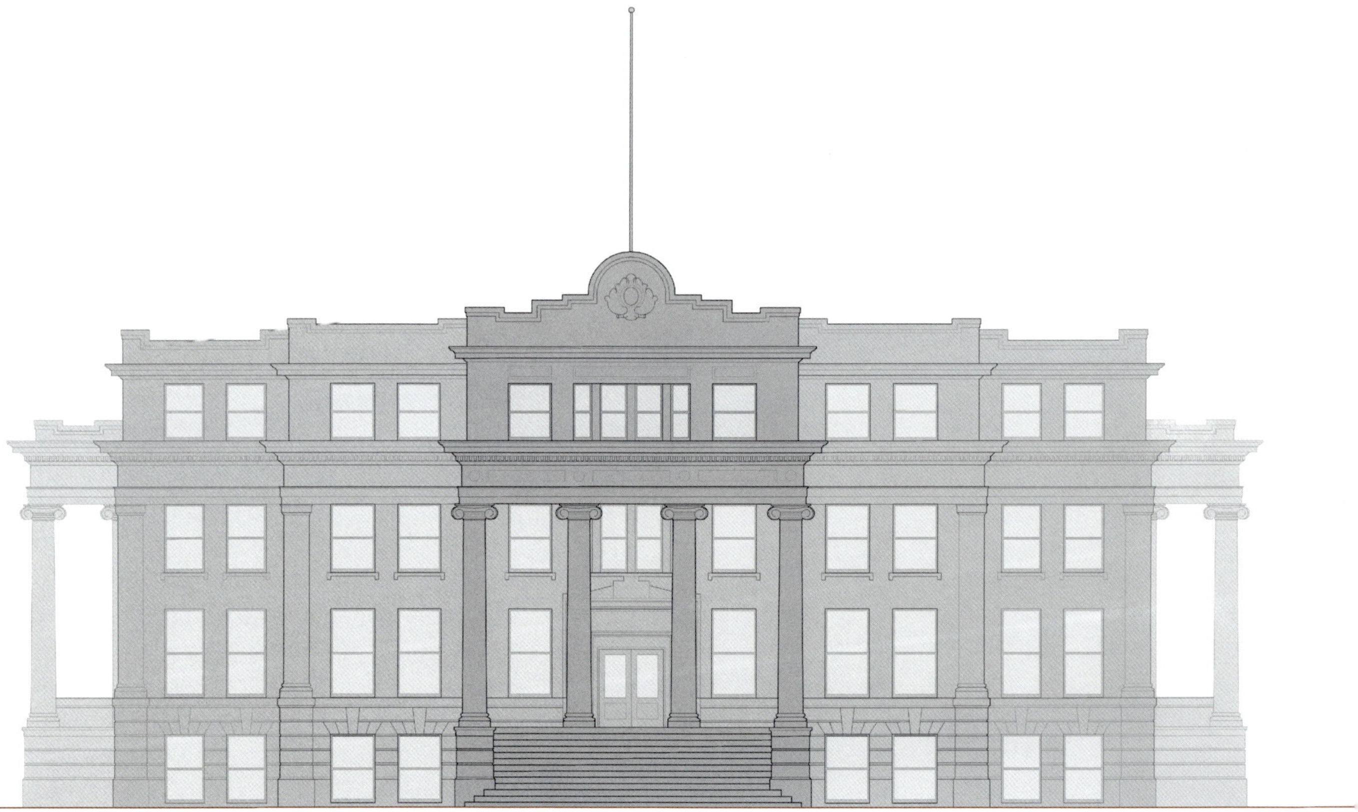

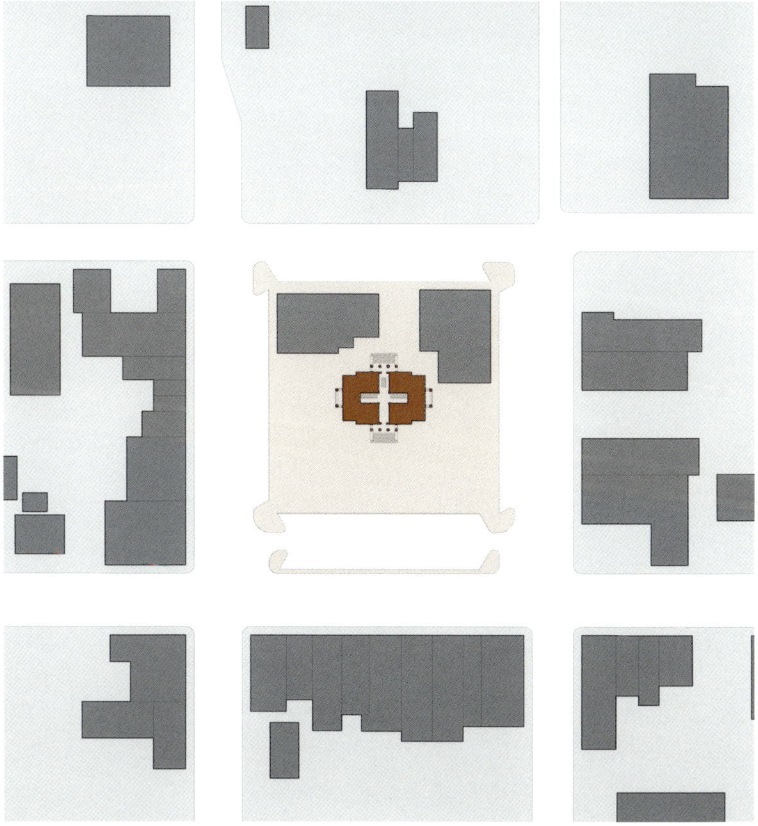

COUNTY ESTABLISHED: 1851

2010 POPULATION: 19,816

1919: built, William R. Kaufman

SIMILAR TO: Dallam, Lynn

Several different architects throughout the state used courthouse designs similar to the one in Freestone County. In each example, the ground floor is treated like a base, with monumental stairs on the building's broader sides leading up to the main level. Less prominent stairs lead to the basement level on the building's two shorter sides.

Although the rules of classical proportions limited the columns to two stories, the space requirements necessitated three floors. As was often the case with designs executed in the Beaux-Arts style, an attic story was added above the cornice to properly balance the composition. The building's parapet was stepped, both in plan and elevation, to accentuate its perceived depth.

1924 Limestone County

GROESBECK, TEXAS

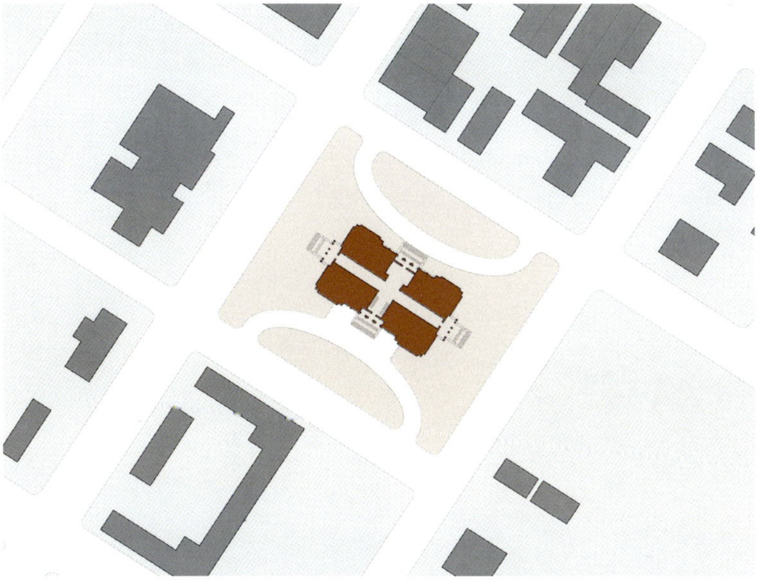

COUNTY ESTABLISHED: 1841
2010 POPULATION: 23,384

1924: built, Rockwell H. Stuckey

SIMILAR TO: Live Oak, Stephens

A double-story colonnade gives the broad main façade of the Limestone County Courthouse its monumentality. This building-as-colonnade motif enjoyed a brief period of popularity in government buildings during the 1920s, representing an alternative to the vertical dome or tower of previous eras. The large circular drives that lead to the main entrances in Limestone County speak to the growing influence the automobile was beginning to have on courthouse design.

Despite what is implied by the county's name, the Limestone County Courthouse was built of brick. This dark masonry, along with its cast-concrete detailing elements, can be seen in other courthouses built at this time, including those in Atascosa, Mills, and Freestone Counties.

1926 Kerr County

KERRVILLE, TEXAS

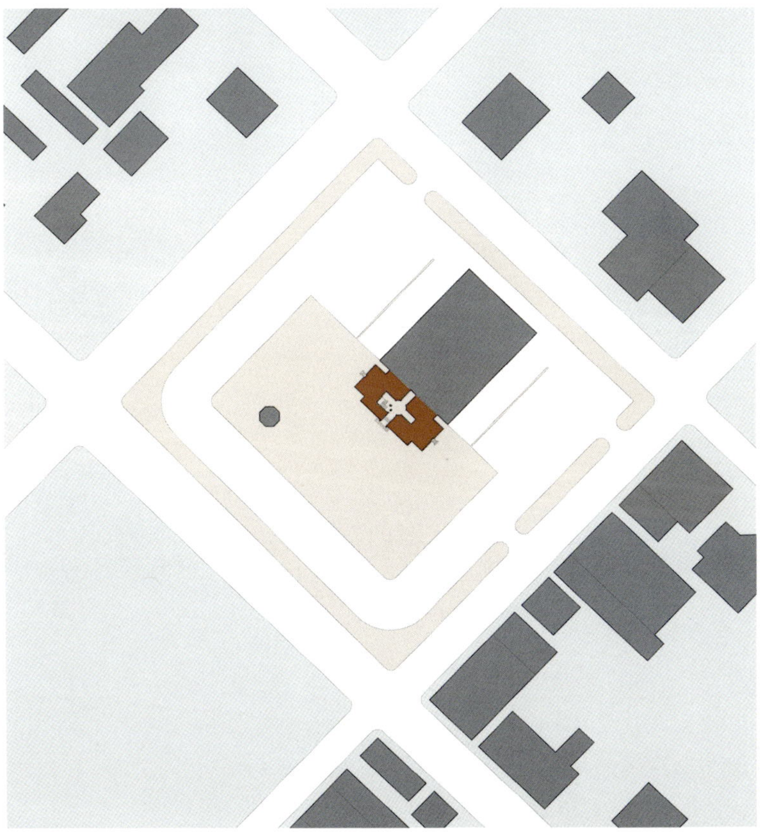

COUNTY ESTABLISHED: 1856
2010 POPULATION: 49,625

1926: built, Adams and Adams

SIMILAR TO: Bailey

The Kerr County Courthouse exists as a brick mass, with restrained stone detailing provided to give the building a Beaux-Arts flavor. The mass is eroded at the corners to give the building a distinctive profile. Because of the large size of the city blocks in Kerrville, the courthouse appears diminutive on its square and does not possess the same dominant presence exerted by other courthouses in the state.

A large annex was added to the northeast side of the courthouse, and although this destroyed one of the primary façades of the original courthouse, it allowed its front façade to remain intact even as the facility grew in size.

1927 Uvalde County

UVALDE, TEXAS

COUNTY ESTABLISHED: 1856
2010 POPULATION: 26,405

1927: built, Henry T. Phelps

SIMILAR TO: Brown, Mills, Wood

The rectangular form of the Uvalde County Courthouse is accentuated by grand porticos on its east and west façades. The integration of these elements is quite sophisticated, with the play of brick and limestone creating a cohesive composition. That composition is predominantly horizontal in its orientation, giving the building a staid presence.

The courthouse square sits within an expansive civic center in downtown Uvalde. Three blocks are occupied by the courthouse, city hall, and post office, while the fourth is left as an open park. The generosity of this planning gesture is remarkable given Uvalde's relatively small size.

1927

Burleson County

CALDWELL, TEXAS

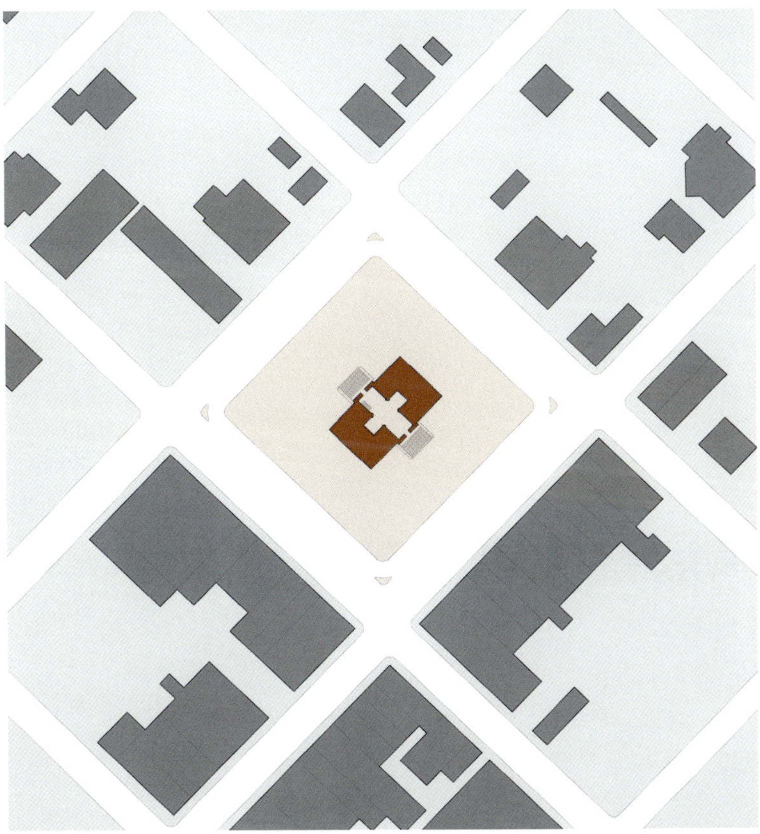

COUNTY ESTABLISHED: 1846
2010 POPULATION: 17,187

1927: built, J. M. Glover

SIMILAR TO: Cameron, Mills, Willacy

The brick Burleson County Courthouse sits at the summit of a pronounced hill in the small town of Caldwell. As in other courthouses of its era, the main floor of this courthouse is raised above a partially sunken basement story. Entrances lead to this basement level on the shorter façades, while monumental stairs climb to the courthouse's elevated first level on the main façades. This gesture provides a heightened sense of arrival to the structure.

Despite considerable articulation of the individual façades, these classical details are remarkably flat in overall depth.[19] Shadows do little to animate the building over the course of the day.

1930

Travis County

AUSTIN, TEXAS

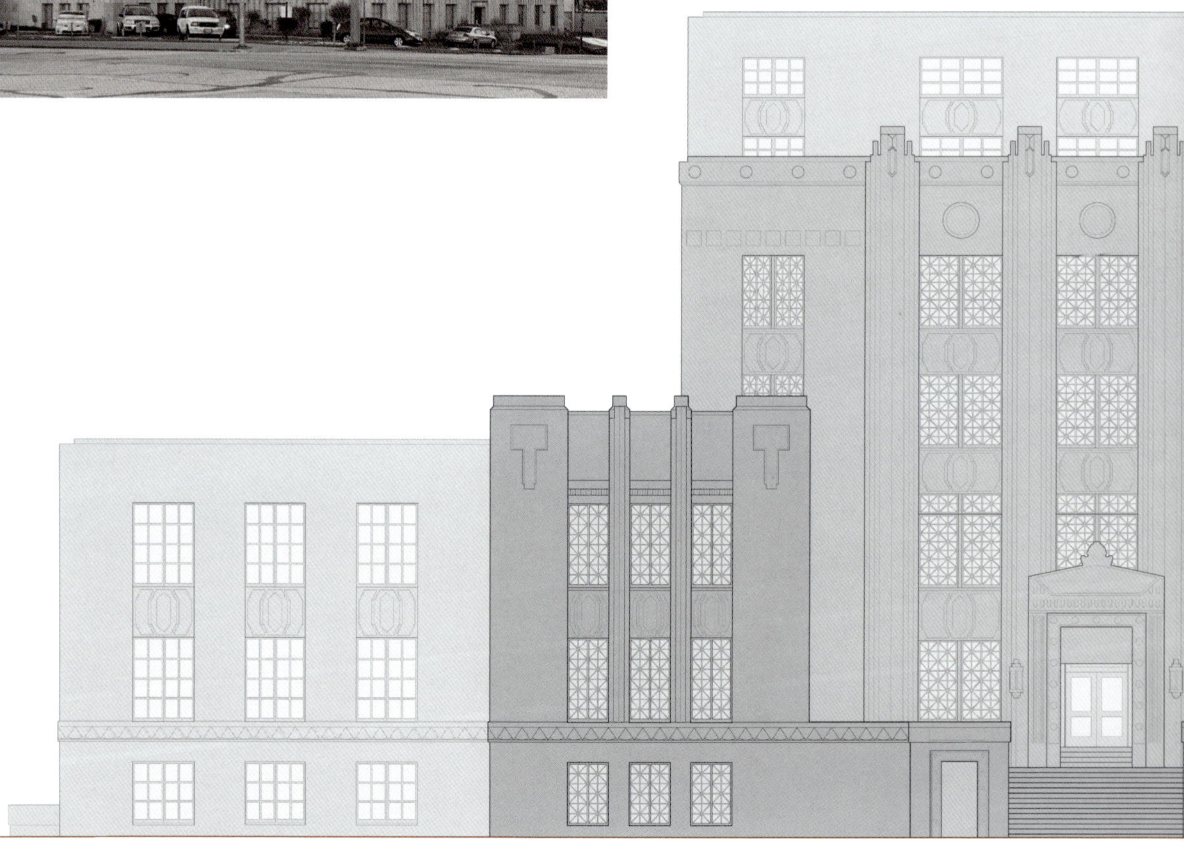

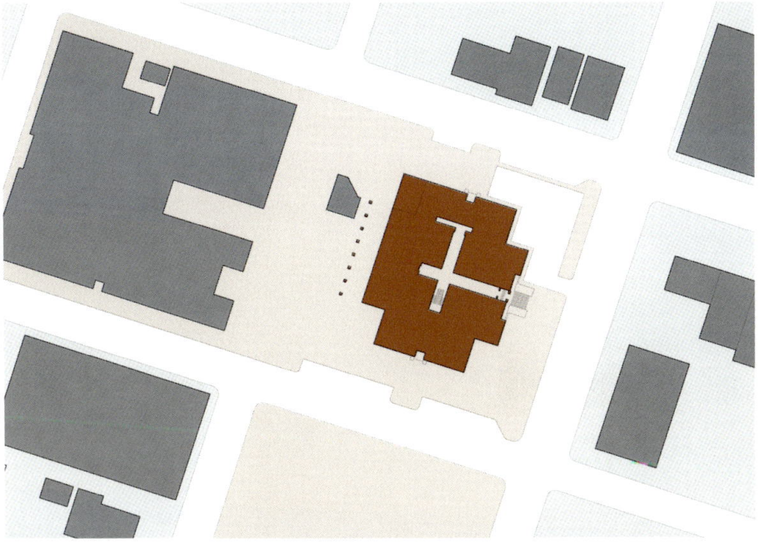

COUNTY ESTABLISHED: 1840
2010 POPULATION: 1,024,266

1930: built, Page Brothers
1959/1962: significant additions

SIMILAR TO: none

Although additions to the Travis County Courthouse remained sympathetic to the details of the original building, the elegant proportions of its initial massing have been lost. While many Depression-era courthouses contained similar stylistic motifs, in the Travis County Courthouse these details are given a degree of formal expression not seen elsewhere. From the abstracted egg-and-dart motifs to the carved friezes over the main entrance, the skill of the masons working on the Travis County Courthouse is worthy of note.

From an urban standpoint, Austin focuses its attention on the Texas State Capitol, with the Travis County Courthouse relegated to a smaller quadrant of its downtown grid.

1935 Guadalupe County

SEGUIN, TEXAS

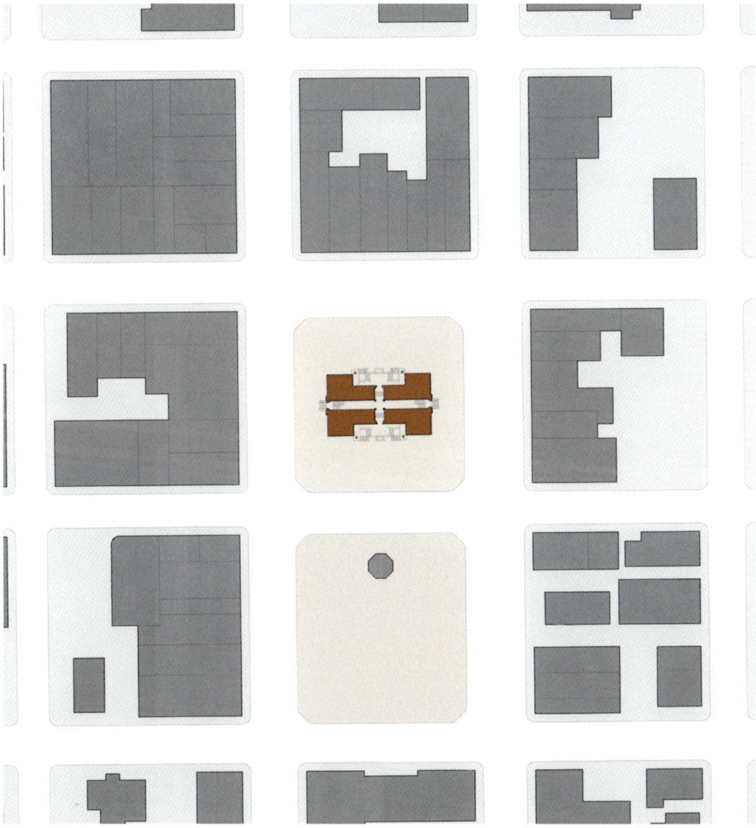

COUNTY ESTABLISHED: 1846
2010 POPULATION: 131,533

1935: built, Wirtz and Calhoun

SIMILAR TO: Chambers, Liberty, Houston, Van Zandt

The Depression-era Guadalupe County Courthouse is configured so that its two projecting wings frame entry courts on the north and south sides of the building. These courts are made even more formal by the addition of framed steps leading to the entry doors. Art deco sculptures of figures representing "wisdom" and "justice" are framed above the building's entries. "Wisdom" is shown to be a man, while "justice," rather predictably, is a blindfolded woman. Unlike her male companion, she is fully clothed. These ceremonial entryways have recently been closed in response to security and accessibility demands. The current entry sequence now requires visitors to pass through secondary doors that lead down into the building's basement.

Although the limestone courthouse itself is bilaterally symmetrical with identical north and south elevations, its urban condition is not as balanced. The courthouse square is located adjacent to Seguin's Central Park, giving the courthouse's southern façade considerably more civic importance.

1936

Burnet County

BURNET, TEXAS

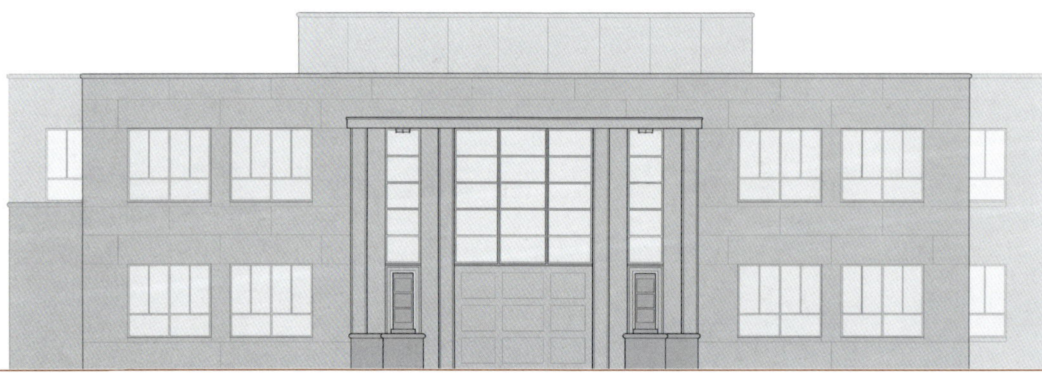

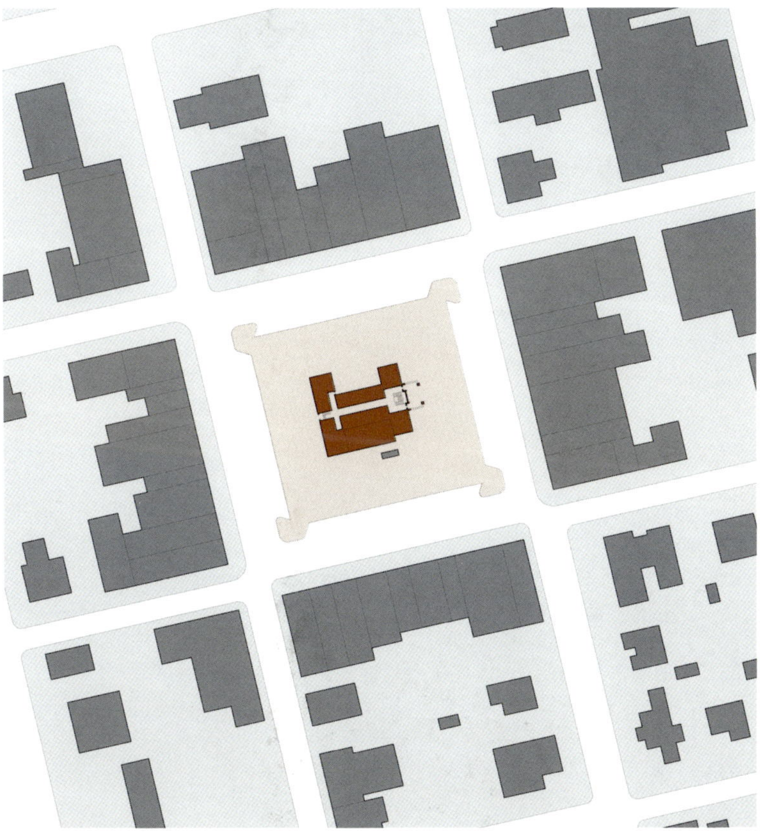

COUNTY ESTABLISHED: 1852
2010 POPULATION: 42,750

1936: built, Wirtz and Calhoun
2011: restored (THCPP), 1113 Architects

SIMILAR TO: Gaines

Decimated by the collapse of agricultural prices following the US stock market crash in 1929, Burnet County first received federal aid in the form of a WPA dam project. County officials were next able to secure federal funds to replace their 1874 courthouse. Although the new courthouse was built at the same time as others throughout the state, this granite-clad courthouse lacks the familiar massing and detailing of its limestone contemporaries.

The layout of the Burnet County Courthouse closely resembles that of the Wilson County Courthouse, which was designed over fifty years earlier. Like the structure in Floresville, the courthouse in Burnet originally featured an I-shaped plan and an entry lobby. But where the 1884 Wilson County Courthouse has a tower designating its main entry, Burnet County's courthouse has a vaguely Egyptian, nine-panel bas-relief sculpture.

1939 Comanche County

COMANCHE, TEXAS

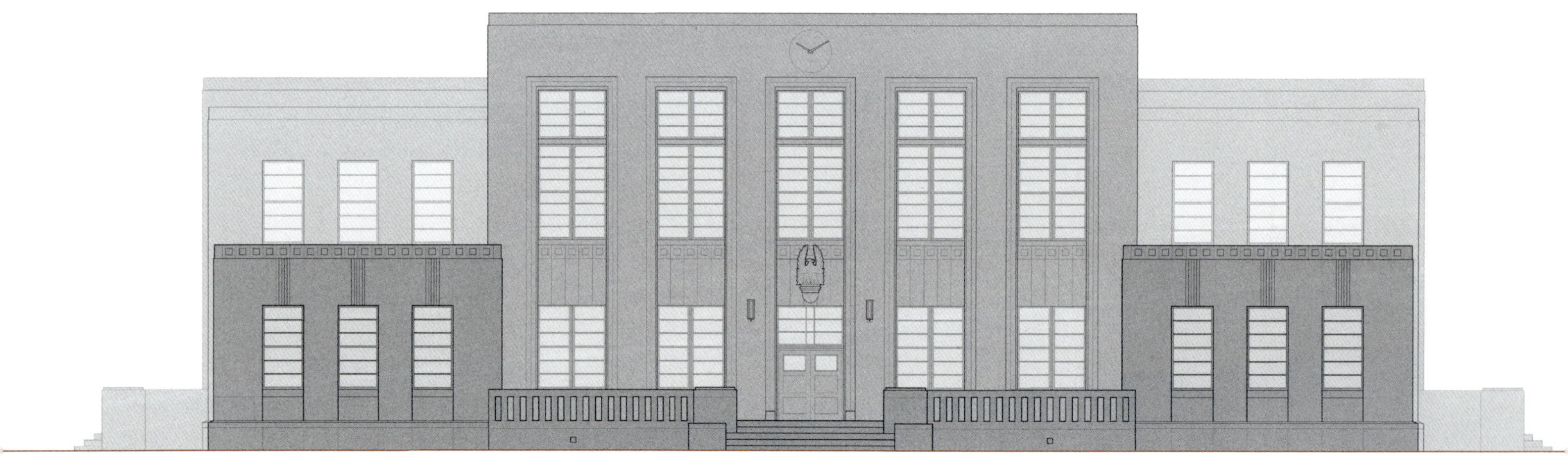

COUNTY ESTABLISHED: 1856
2010 POPULATION: 13,974

1939: built, Wyatt C. Hendrick

SIMILAR TO: Cherokee

Most Depression-era courthouses in Central Texas were built as a series of cubic volumes that have been subtly shifted relative to one another. This is the case in Comanche County, except that here these volumes are faced in limestone that is roughly finished. This represents a regional take on the smoother stone of other courthouses built in the 1930s.

The 1939 courthouse replaced a structure dating from 1890 that was almost identical to the courthouse in Milam County. The county's first courthouse, a partially reconstructed log cabin structure dating from 1859, sits on a corner of the current square as an example of the primitive nature of many pre–Civil War courthouses in Texas.

1939 Gillespie County

FREDERICKSBURG, TEXAS

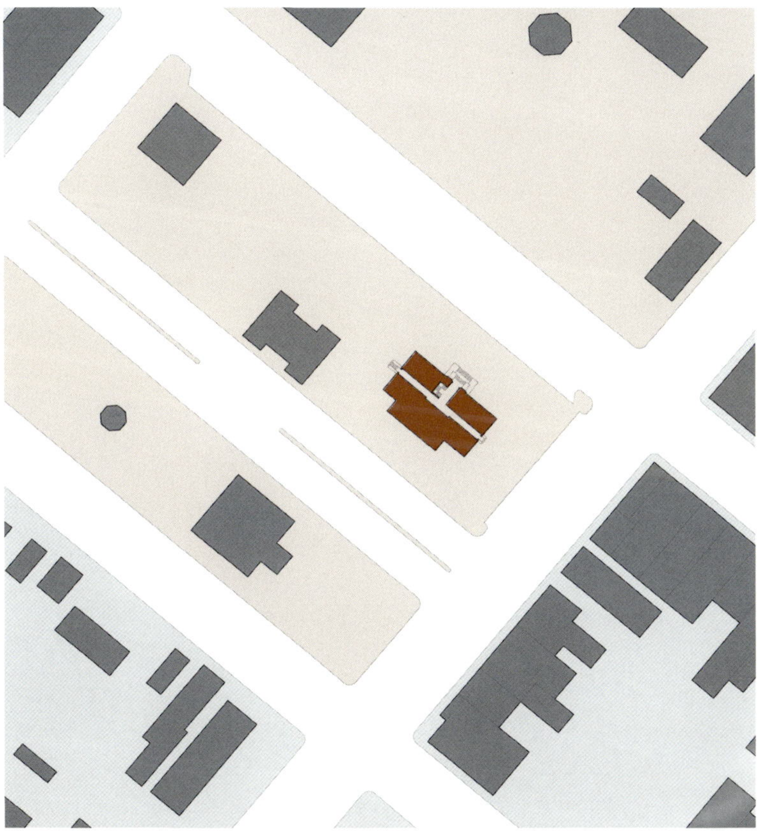

COUNTY ESTABLISHED: 1848
2010 POPULATION: 24,837

1939: built, Edward Stein

SIMILAR TO: Borden, Falls

Although Public Works Administration funding was secured for the construction of the Gillespie County Courthouse, a local architect was given the commission. Stein's design is a respectable example of brick Depression-era modernistic architecture, even though it makes no reference to the unique architectural character of Fredericksburg. In a town known for its distinctively German limestone buildings, the brick courthouse feels strangely foreign.

The county's 1882 former courthouse by Alfred Giles still sits directly opposite the reconstructed octagonal Vereins Kirche building that once acted as the cultural center of Fredericksburg. Although it was not torn down, the 1882 courthouse did fall into disrepair after it was decommissioned. It was restored in 1967 and now serves as a public library.

1939

Falls County

MARLIN, TEXAS

COUNTY ESTABLISHED: 1850
2010 POPULATION: 17,866

1939: built, Arthur E. Thomas

SIMILAR TO: Gillespie

The Falls County Courthouse is almost completely obscured by a dense perimeter of live oak trees. Beyond this foliage lies a well-proportioned courthouse with a façade defined by an articulated central entry tower similar to those seen in other Depression-era courthouse designs. Nearly half of the funds used for the construction of the courthouse were provided by federal Public Works Administration grants.

Unlike those of other courthouses from the era, the windows of this courthouse are framed between limestone pilasters that do not visibly support a cornice. The corner pilasters are thickened and fluted to give the entire composition a more sturdy appearance.

1939 Washington County

BRENHAM, TEXAS

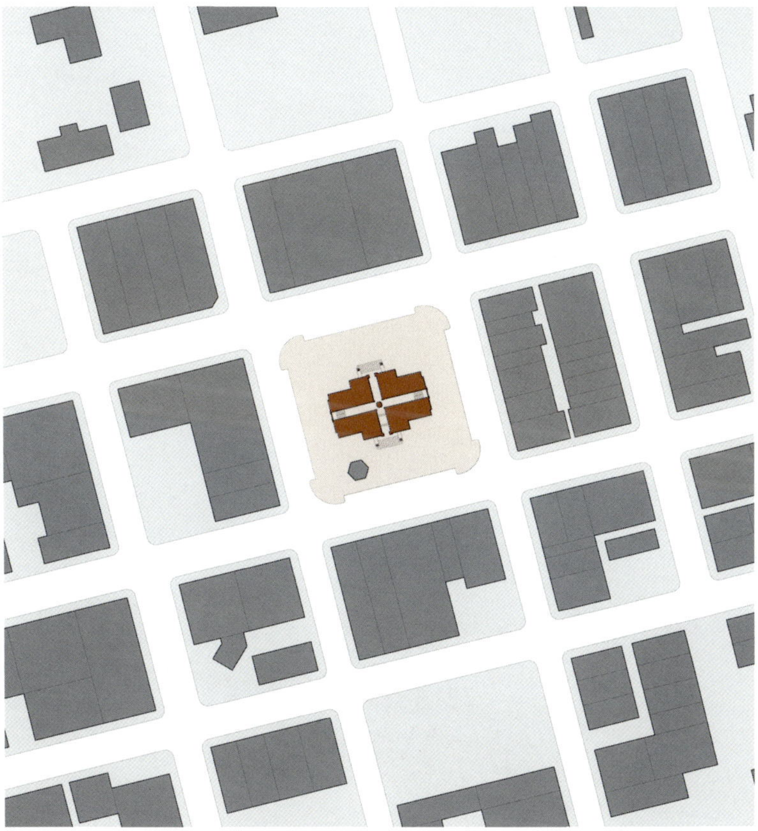

COUNTY ESTABLISHED: 1836
2010 POPULATION: 33,718

1939: built, Hedrick and Lindsay / Travis Broesche

SIMILAR TO: Gregg, Rockwall, Ward

Perceived as a geometrical composition of cubic forms, the courthouse consists of limestone masses animated by a play of light limestone and dark, reflective marble. The composition emphasizes the vertical, with dark spandrel panels articulating the windows as tall strips. The aluminum eagle statuettes standing guard over the building's four entrances are more typically associated with federal facilities.

The city blocks of Brenham are remarkably small, measuring only 160 feet square. This makes for a very compact downtown that serves as a tight frame for the courthouse. Although it has never been restored, the courthouse remains in good condition.

1955

Brazos County

BRYAN, TEXAS

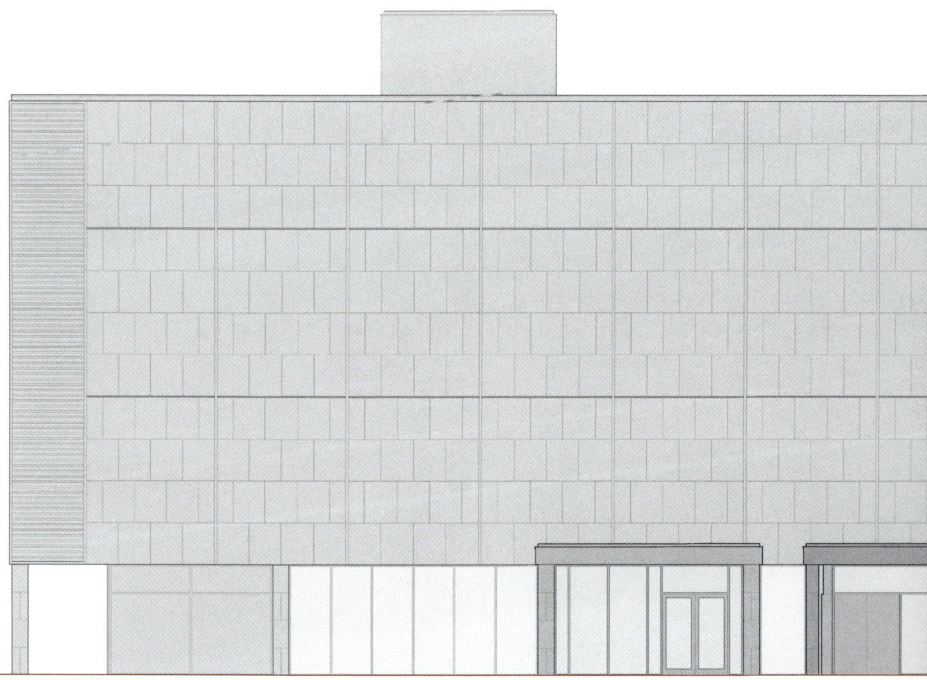

COUNTY ESTABLISHED 1841

2010 POPULATION 194,851

1955: built, Caudill, Rowlett, Scott

1986, 1991: significant additions

SIMILAR TO: Austin

When first completed, the Brazos County Courthouse represented a complete rethinking of the courthouse and its relationship to its square. Rather than existing as an object in a field, the building presented itself as a campus of interconnected buildings. Judicial functions requiring greater security were located in a four-story, marble-clad slab, while offices requiring greater connectivity to the public were organized around a series of exterior courtyards.[20]

In the years since its construction, the open campus plan has been mostly obscured by multiple additions. With the courtyards gone, only the opaque tower remains, rendering illegible the original design intent.

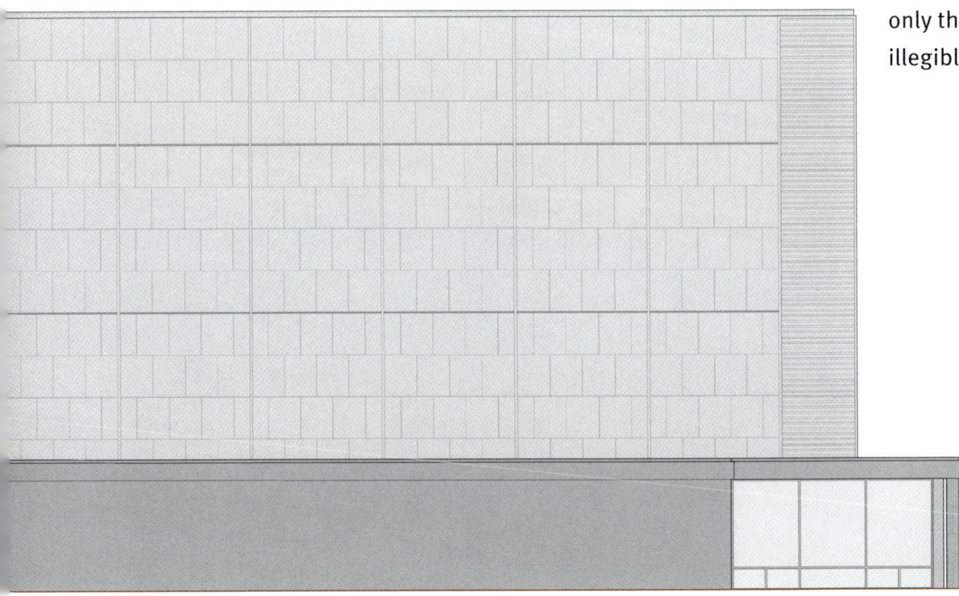

1970 Madison County

MADISONVILLE, TEXAS

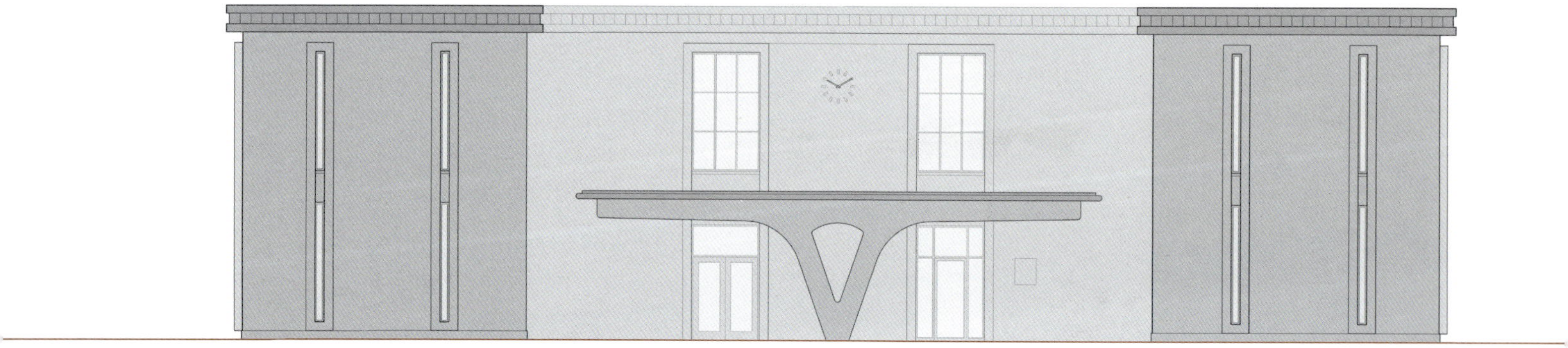

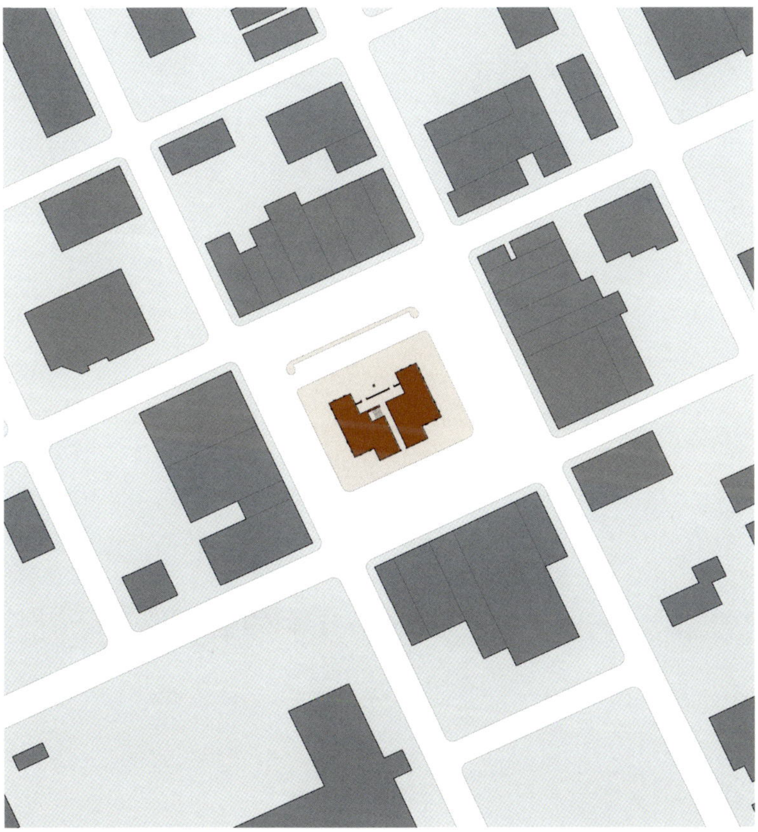

COUNTY ESTABLISHED: 1854
2010 POPULATION: 13,664

1970: built, Dickson, Dickson, Buckley & Bullock

SIMILAR TO: none

With side wings framing a central entry court, the massing of the Madison County Courthouse is formally similar to some Depression-era courthouses. There is, however, little articulation of detail, and the amount of the façade given to windows is exceedingly small, resulting in a somewhat prison-like structure. The concrete entry canopy likewise more closely resembles a highway overpass than the entrance to a temple of justice.

Unlike the courthouses of Brazos and Zavala Counties, the courthouse in Madison does not represent a forward-thinking proposition of what a courthouse of the future should be. Rather, it takes a preexisting model, strips away all non-functional ornament, and leaves in its place a practical but otherwise uninspired box.

1970 Zavala County

CRYSTAL CITY, TEXAS

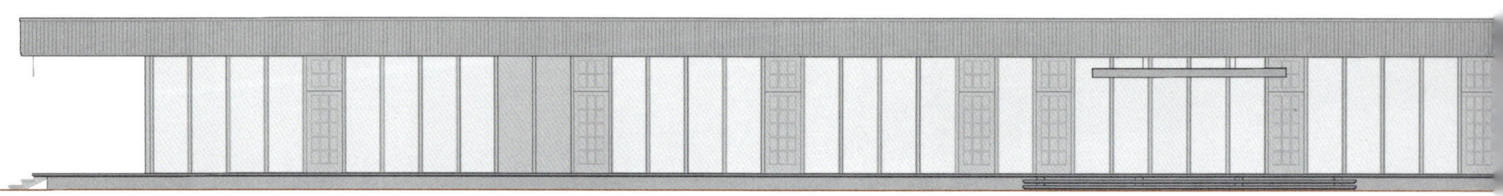

COUNTY ESTABLISHED: 1846
2010 POPULATION: 11,677

1970: built, Gene P. Hobart
1984: significant addition

SIMILAR TO: Martin

Like its modernist cousin in Brazos County, the courthouse in Zavala County is an outlier among Texas county courthouses. Although it was designed with a series of crossing interior corridors, the main public circulation is pushed to a generous covered walkway that defines the building's perimeter.[21] Offices and courtrooms can all be entered directly from this exterior walkway, whose broad overhang shades the building's floor-to-ceiling glazing and contributes to its low horizontal proportions.

This design is informed by Crystal City's warm, subtropical climate, which makes outdoor circulation feasible. The modernist rethinking of the standard courthouse model is compelling, even if contemporary security realities have made this strategy challenging to use.

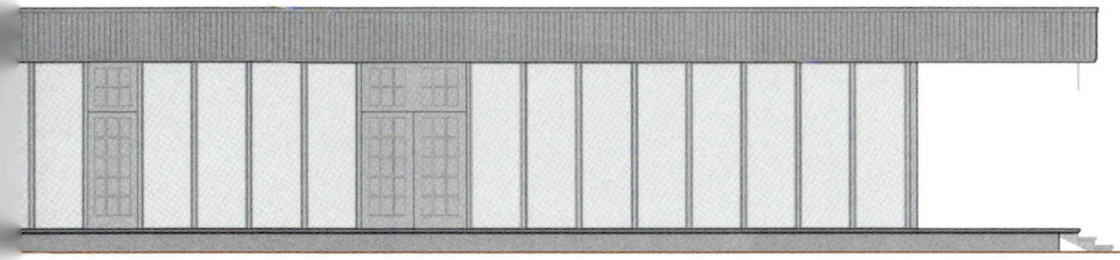

THE ARCHITECTS

Despite the large physical size of central Texas, a relatively small number of architects competed against one another for the same courthouse commissions. The backgrounds of these architects are as varied as the courthouses they designed. Alfred Giles (1853–1920) came from a privileged background and was born and educated in England before moving to Texas for health reasons. Oscar Ruffini (1858–1957) was born in Cleveland and worked for the architect of the Texas State Capitol before setting up a practice of his own in San Angelo. J. Riely Gordon (1863–1937) moved to Texas from Virginia in his youth, and despite having no formal architectural training, quickly rose to be the predominant courthouse architect of his time. Henry T. Phelps (1871–1944) was born in Texas and spent the entirety of his professional career in San Antonio.

Counties typically selected architects not by their qualifications but through design competitions that required architects to submit detailed construction drawings and specifications. Once the commission was awarded, the architect would have only a few months to complete the drawings and incorporate any modifications requested by the county. Developing unique designs for multiple competitions was a risky and expensive proposition for the architects involved. It made better business sense to submit a variation of a previously developed scheme.[22]

As the functional requirements of one county would

Lampasas County Courthouse, 1883, Lampasas, Texas

Lampasas County Courthouse, 1883, Lampasas, Texas

Hill County Courthouse, 1890, Hillsboro, Texas

vary only slightly from those of another, it followed that an architect's design solutions for multiple counties would be similar as well. W. C. Dodson produced close to twenty variations on his standard courthouse design, which featured an elaborate tower and Second-Empire details.[23] Dodson created what was essentially a design template that could be scaled up or down to accommodate a range of program and budget levels.

Upon first glance, J. Riely Gordon seems to be like Dodson in that he spent the better part of the 1890s recycling the same basic floor plan for multiple counties. Upon closer inspection, the arc of Gordon's designs reveals a sustained development of a unique solution to the programmatic and formal requirements of a county courthouse in Texas.[24] Each of his projects can be understood as a deliberate step in a larger iterative design process. In all, eighteen courthouses were built in Texas to Gordon's designs, a third of which still exist in central Texas. A survey of these projects shows a number of distinct developmental phases as well as the evolution of his distinctive plan. Early outliers gave way to experimentation with an open courtyard scheme before this was condensed into his signature cruciform courthouse design. Even while working within the parameters of predefined architectural styles, Gordon devised innovative spatial and formal solutions that proved to be highly influential.[25]

The remarkable thing about Gordon, Dodson, and the others is the degree to which they were able to adapt contemporary trends to the specific physical and symbolic needs of a county courthouse in Texas. In doing so they created a collection of built landmarks that still have the power to define and inspire their communities over a century after they were built.

Aransas County Courthouse, 1890 (reconstructed), Rockport, Texas

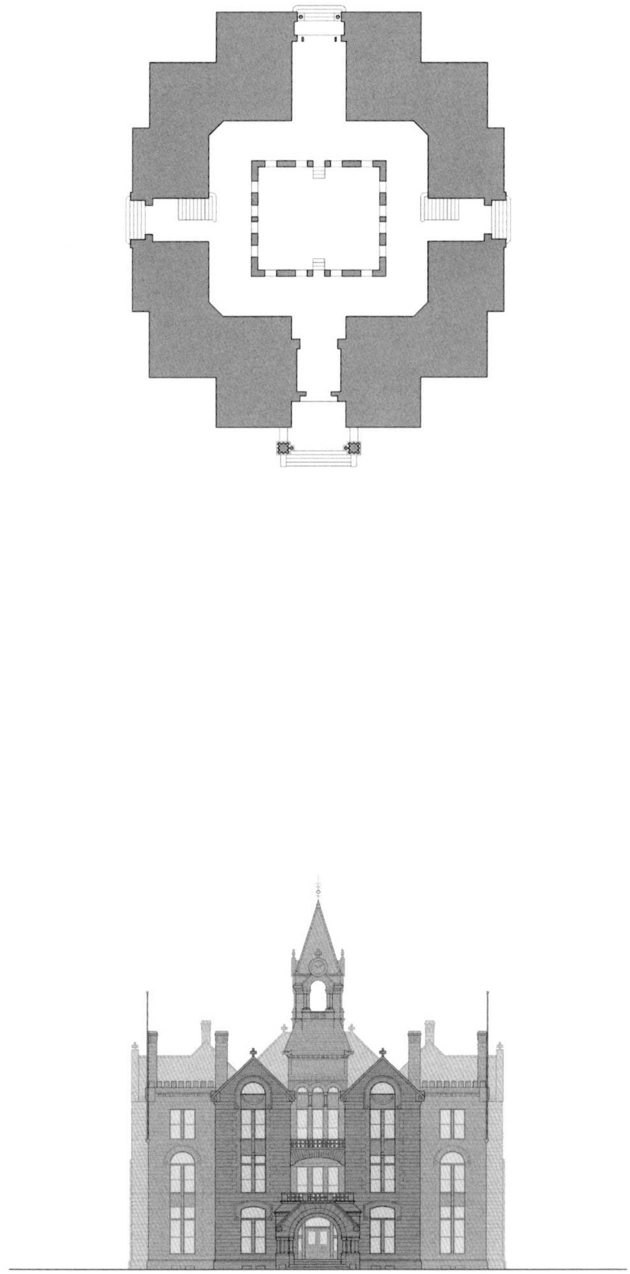

Fayette County Courthouse, 1891, La Grange, Texas

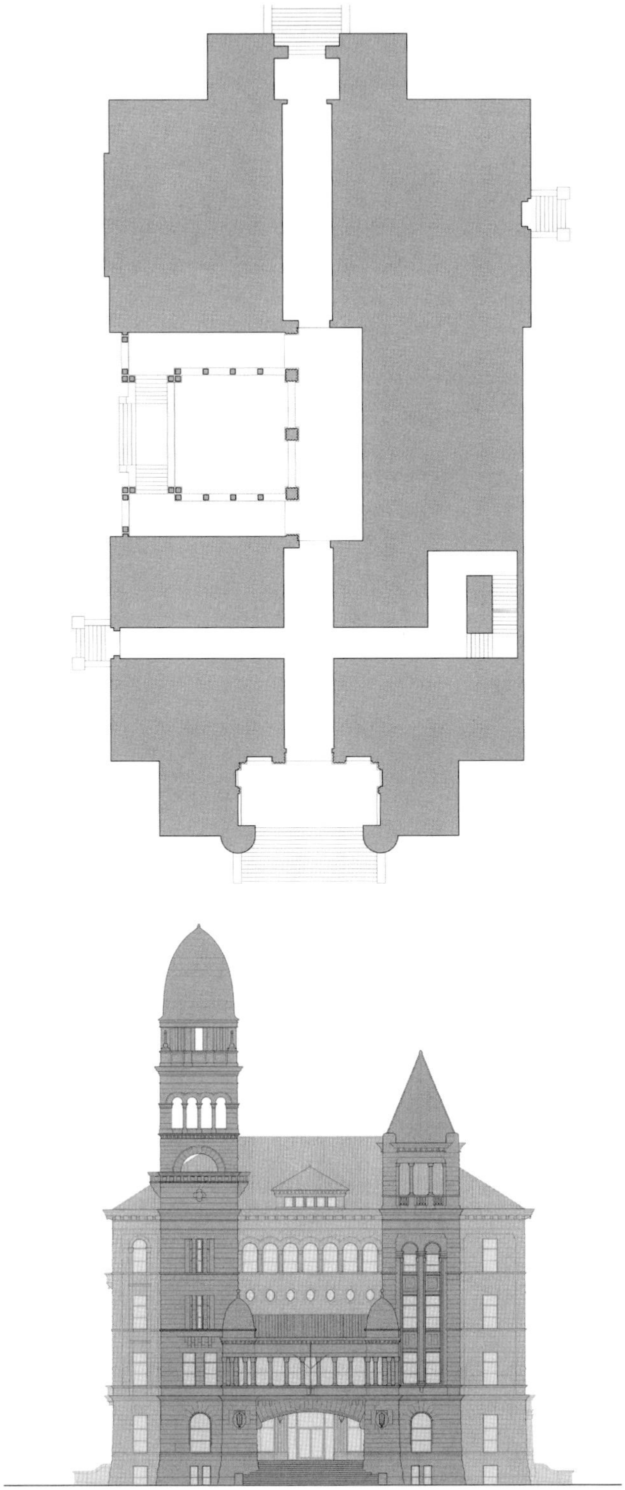

Bexar County Courthouse, 1896, San Antonio, Texas

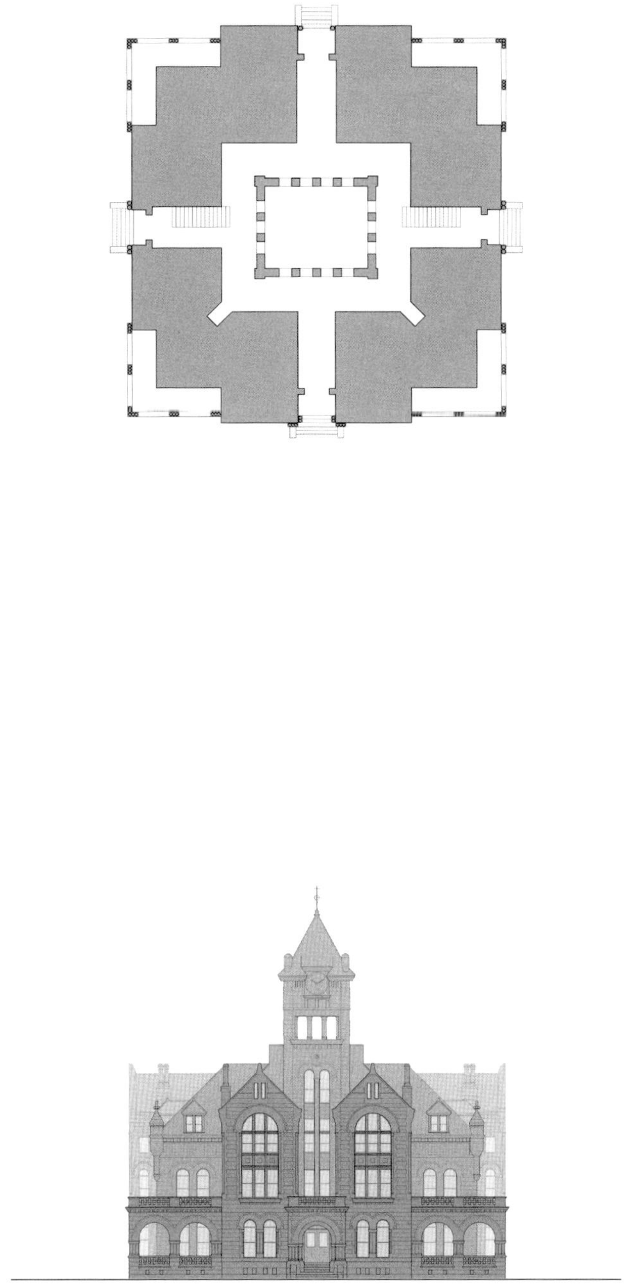

Victoria County Courthouse, 1892, Victoria, Texas

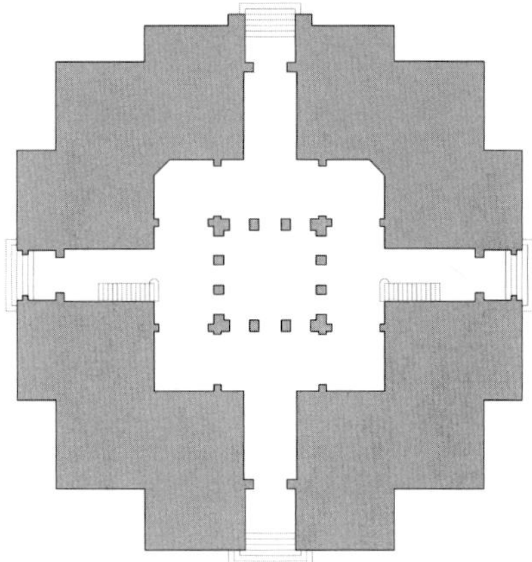

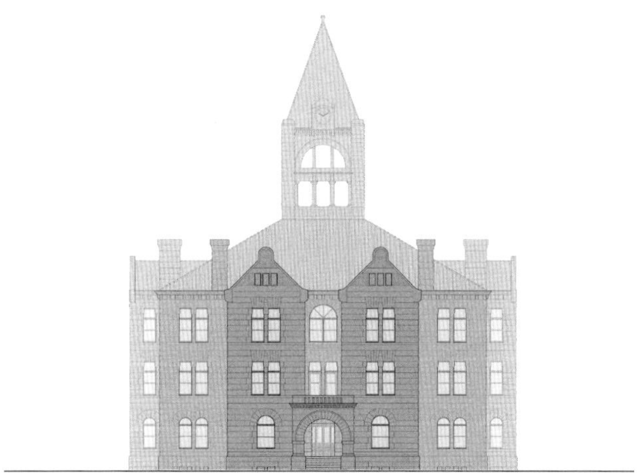

Erath County Courthouse, 1892, Stephenville, Texas

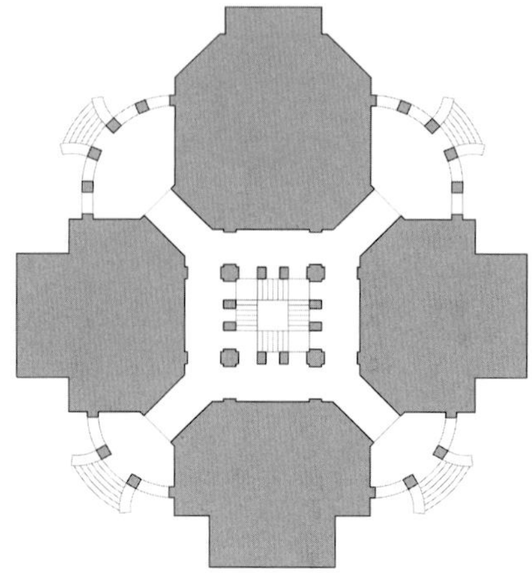

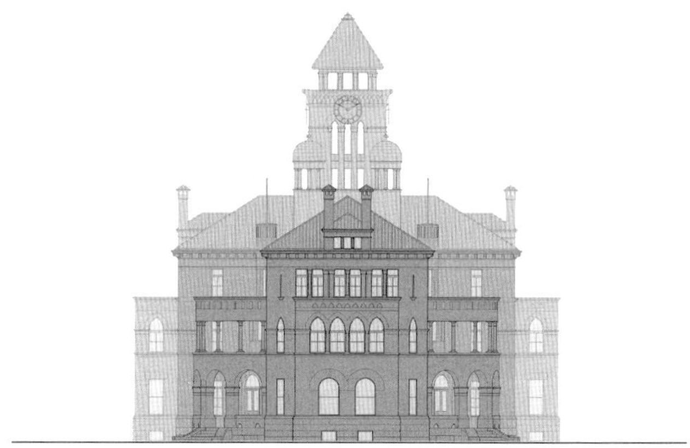

Gonzales County Courthouse, 1894, Gonzales, Texas

Brazoria County Courthouse, 1895 (reconstructed), Brazoria, Texas

Hopkins County Courthouse, 1895, Sulphur Springs, Texas

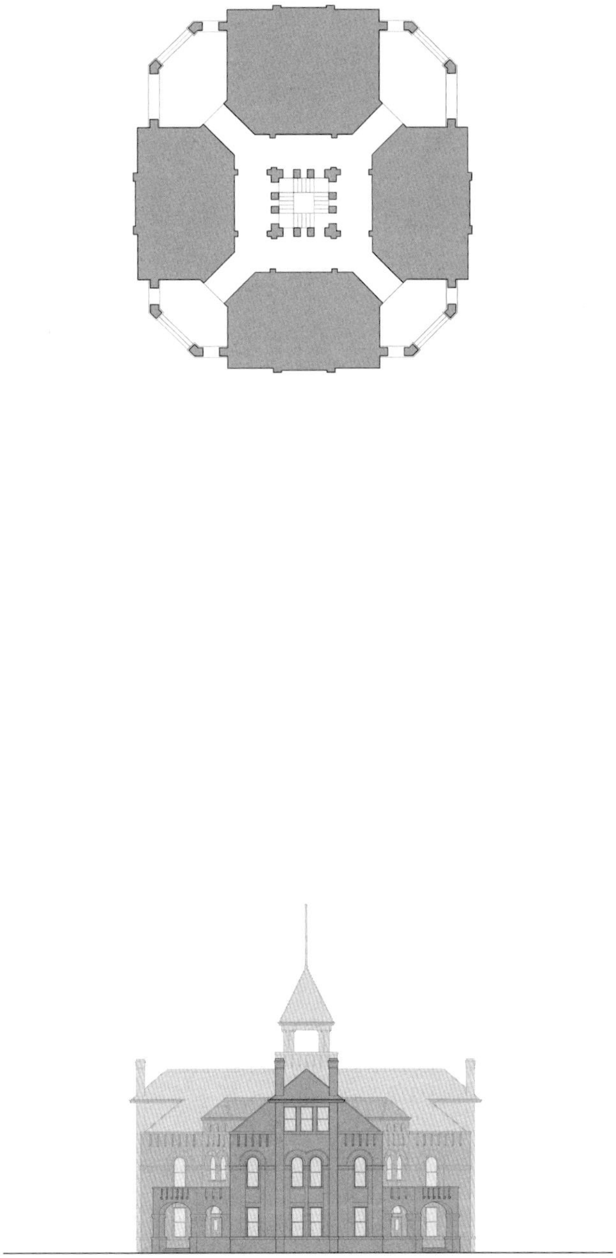

San Patricio County Courthouse, 1895 (reconstructed), Sinton, Texas

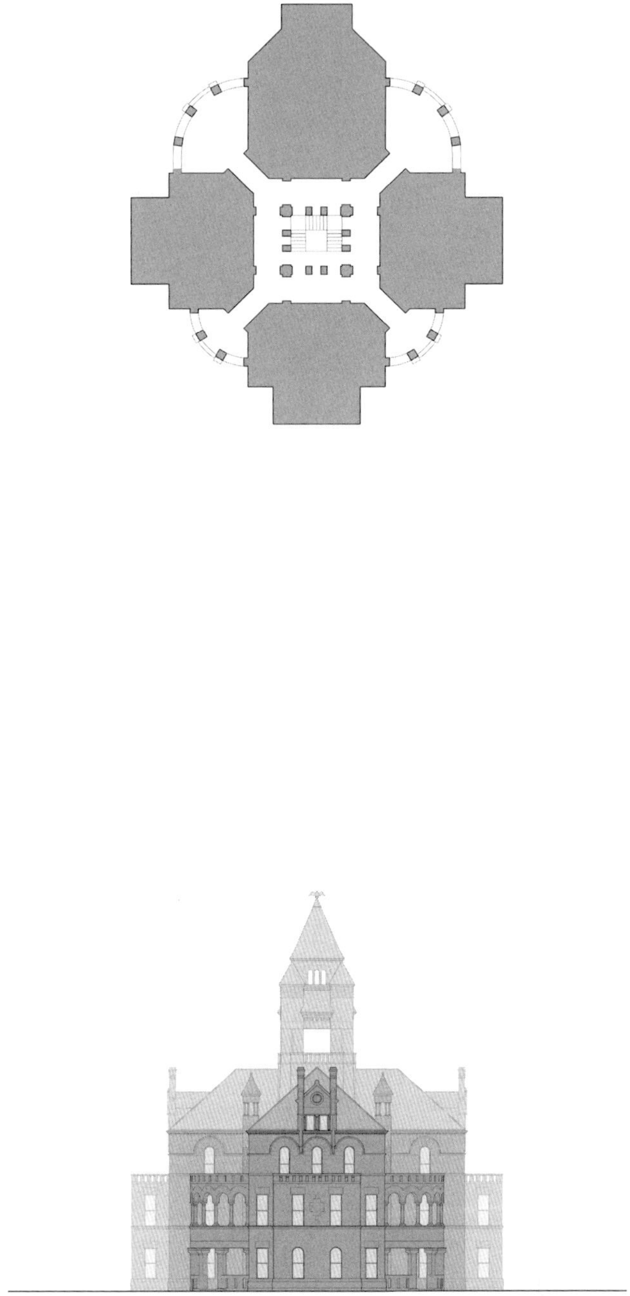

Van Zandt County Courthouse, 1896 (reconstructed), Canton, Texas

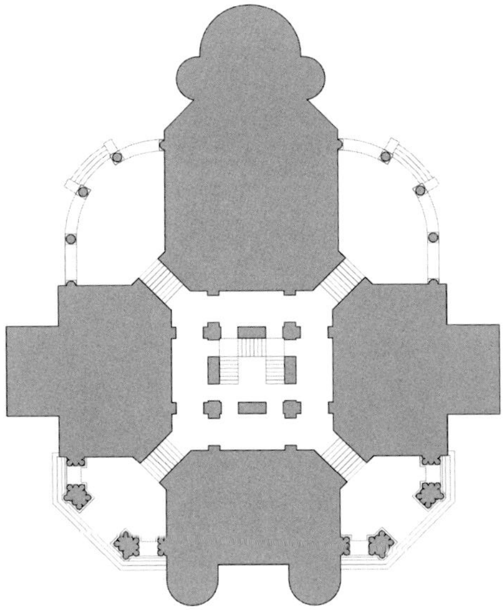

Ellis County Courthouse, 1897, Waxahachie, Texas

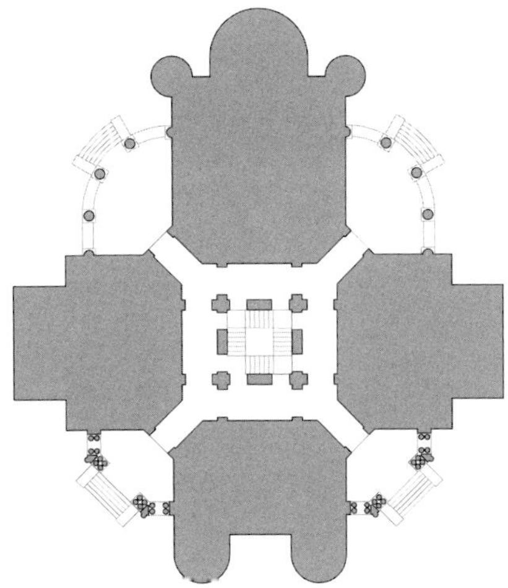

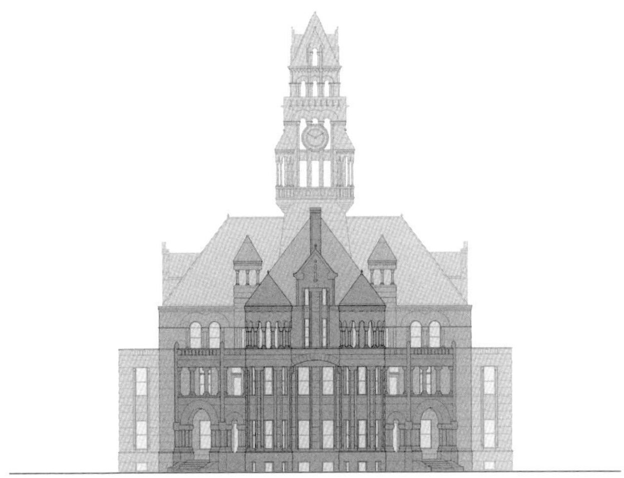

Wise County Courthouse, 1897, Decatur, Texas

Comal County Courthouse, 1898, New Braunfels, Texas

Lee County Courthouse, 1899, Giddings, Texas

Callahan County Courthouse, 1900 (reconstructed), Baird, Texas

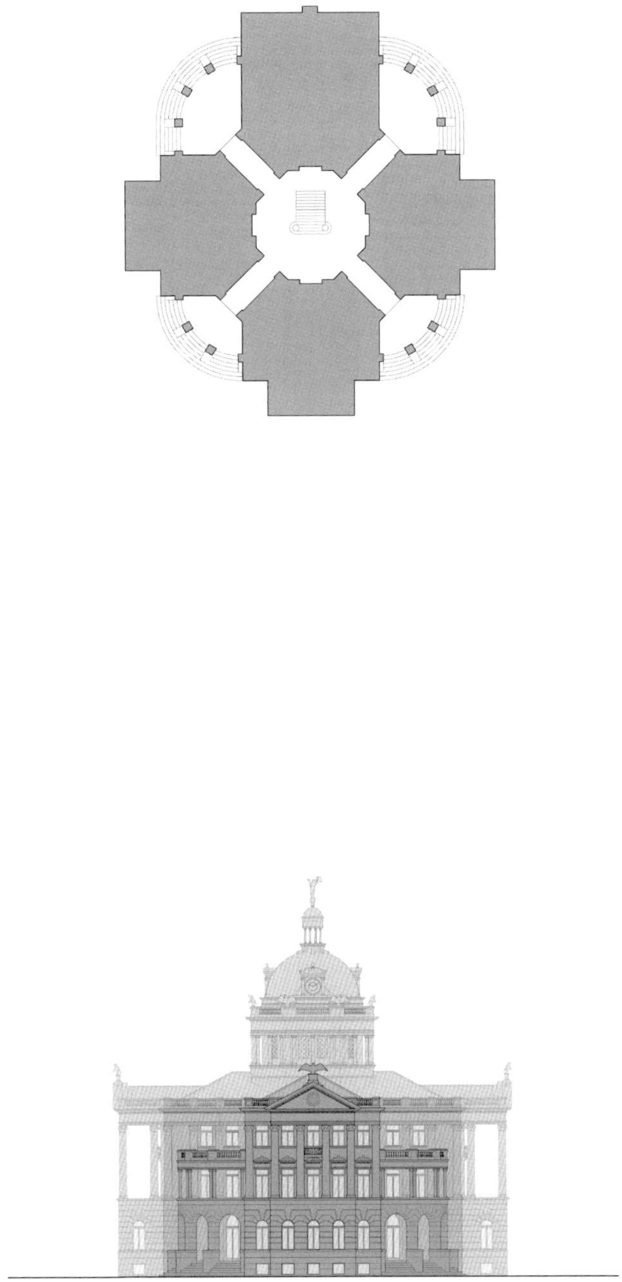

Harrison County Courthouse, 1901, Marshall, Texas

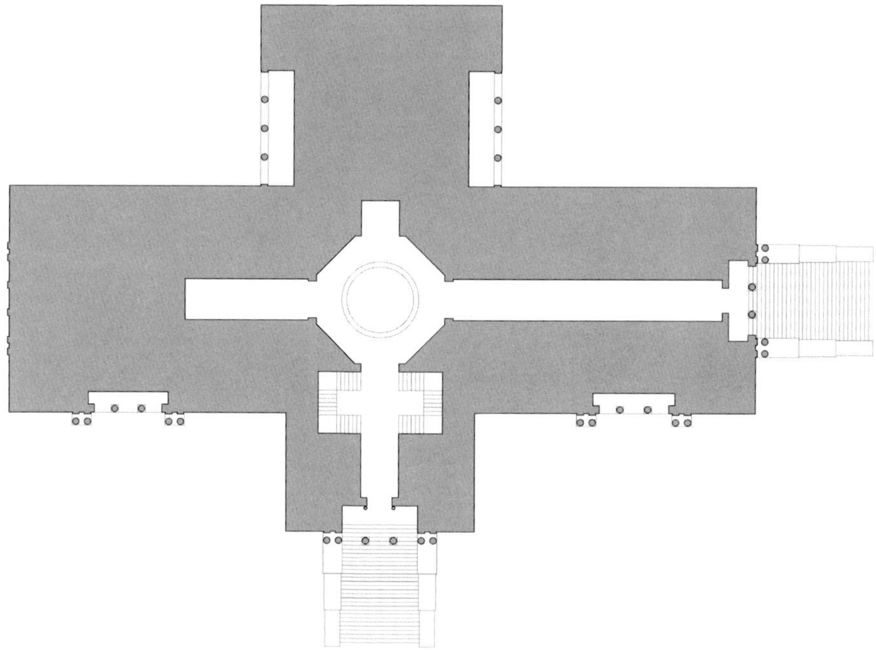

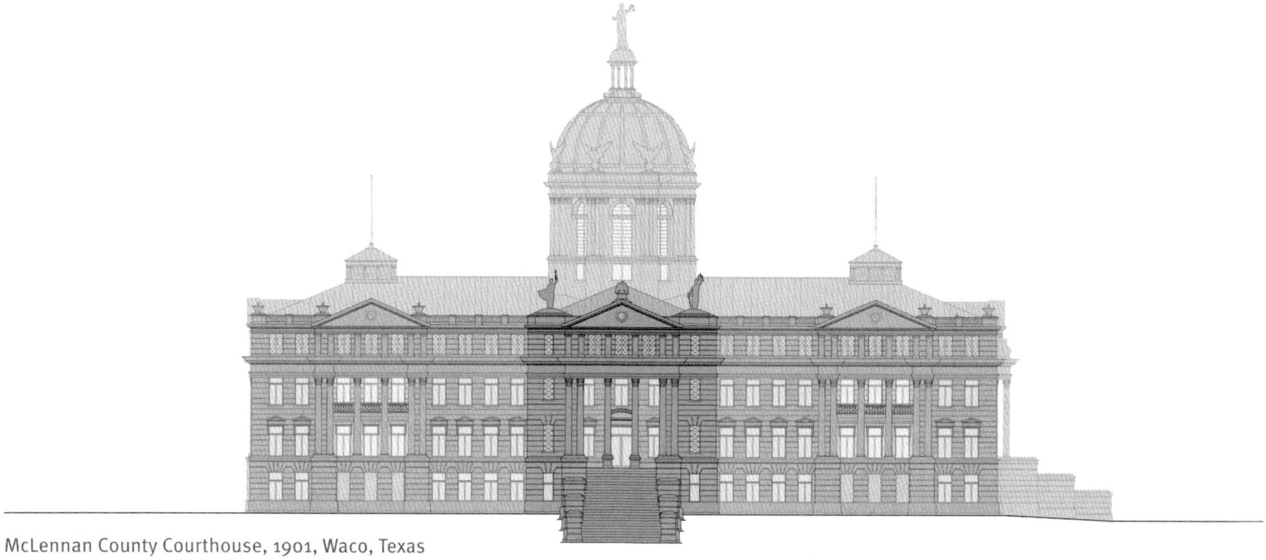

McLennan County Courthouse, 1901, Waco, Texas

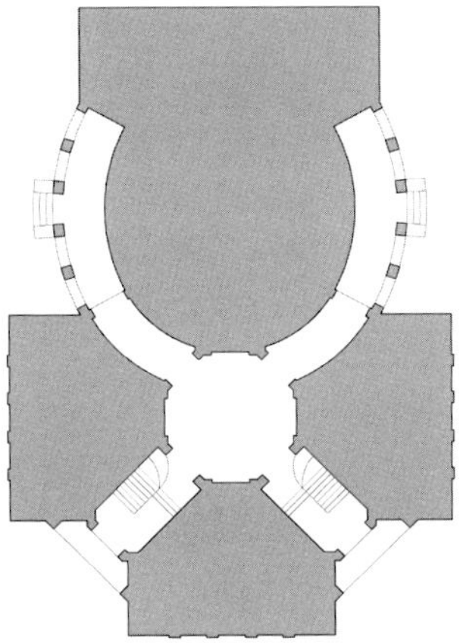

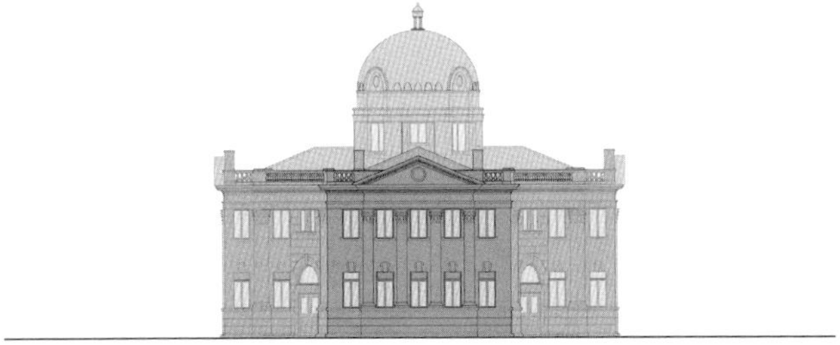

Angelina County Courthouse, 1902 (reconstructed), Lufkin, Texas

Lee County Courthouse, 1899, Giddings, Texas

Conclusions

The physical act of creating a representation of a building through the assembly of lines reveals patterns and relationships that might otherwise go unnoticed. The drawings created for this project may clarify objective realities, but by themselves they can obscure other, more subjective ones. Creating a two-dimensional elevation drawing compresses the nuanced spatial and material realities of a building. For example, the elevation drawings of Gordon's cruciform courthouse designs fail to convey the sculptural richness of the actual buildings. When drawn orthographically, the relative proportions of these courthouses seem awkward in a way they do not when experienced in person.

More than those of the other architects of his era, Gordon's courthouses are too spatially complex to be effectively rendered in the type of frontal elevation drawings created for this survey. Rotating the viewing plane of the elevation by forty-five degrees does a better job of communicating their experiential reality, as does shifting to a perspective view. In other designs of lesser virtuosity, the orthographic and perspectival representations do not significantly differ from one another.

As helpful as drawings are in understanding the relationships between the courthouses of central Texas, to understand the depth of their architectural richness, one must visit these buildings in person. The drives between courthouses may be long, but they are worth the effort.

ON SMALL TOWNS AND BIG COURTHOUSES

The towering county courthouse that dominates its small-town setting is a beguiling if somewhat jarring curiosity of the built Texas landscape. Although this urban relationship can be experientially profound, it may seem misguided for a small community to make such a large investment in architectural spectacle. What may appear inappropriate in the context of contemporary population distribution begins to make more sense when seen in light of the demographic realities of more than a century ago.

In 2010, central Texas was dominated by the urban centers of San Antonio and Austin. The populations of the counties in which these cities are located—Bexar and

Lee County Courthouse, 1899, elevation

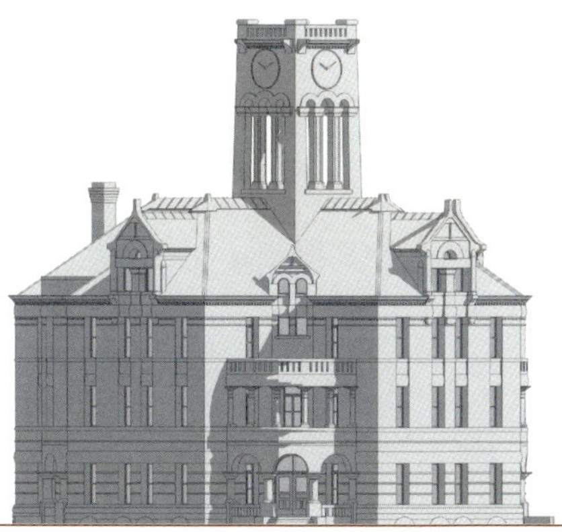

Lee County Courthouse, 1899, rotated elevation

Lee County Courthouse, 1899, perspective

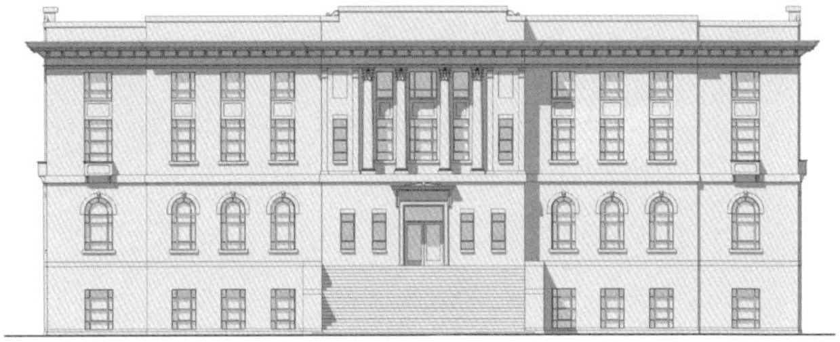

Burleson County Courthouse, 1927, elevation

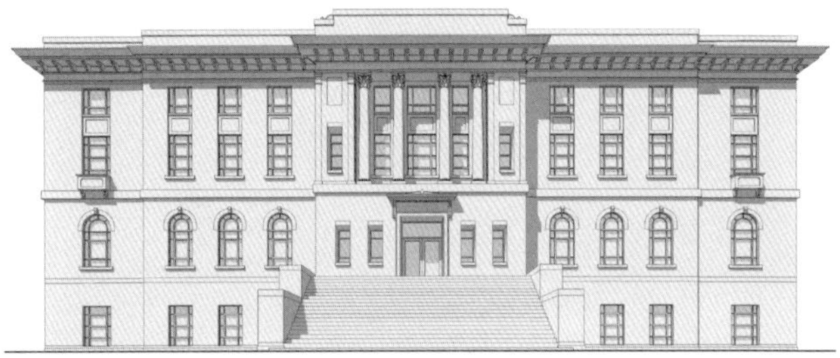

Burleson County Courthouse, 1927, perspective

La Grange, Texas

Travis, respectively—are several orders of magnitude larger than those of other counties in the region. Fayette County, for example, is today one of many rural Texas counties dwarfed by their larger urban cousins. A quarter of the county population of just under 25,000 is concentrated in the county seat of La Grange.

With an older commercial core centered on the courthouse square, La Grange is similar to many other small central Texas towns. One distinguishing characteristic is the massive Romanesque courthouse that dominates its central square. The three-story structure features walls of local and imported stone as well as a clock tower over one hundred feet in height. The building appears to be much more substantial than the size of its community would seem to warrant. Indeed, the courtroom could accommodate a third of the population of La Grange when the building was completed in 1891. Although smaller than the courthouse that would be built a few years later in Bexar County, the Fayette County Courthouse shared similarly grand architectural ambitions.

In 2010, Bexar County was an urban metropolis of 1.7 million people. Fayette County, on the other hand, was a small rural county of 24,554—just a little more than one percent of the population of Bexar. Although Bexar County has always been larger than Fayette, the disparity between the two was not always so great. In 1890 Bexar County was still the largest population center in central Texas, with 49,266 inhabitants, but with a population of 31,481, Fayette County was not that far behind. In 1880 Fayette was in fact the second most populated county in central Texas.

Even though over half of the population of central Texas was concentrated in Bexar and Travis Counties in 2010, in 1890 the population was spread much more evenly among all the counties in the region.

When the Fayette County Commissioners Court decided to build a new courthouse, they had every reason to believe their community would remain one of the state's major population centers. With a constant influx of immi-

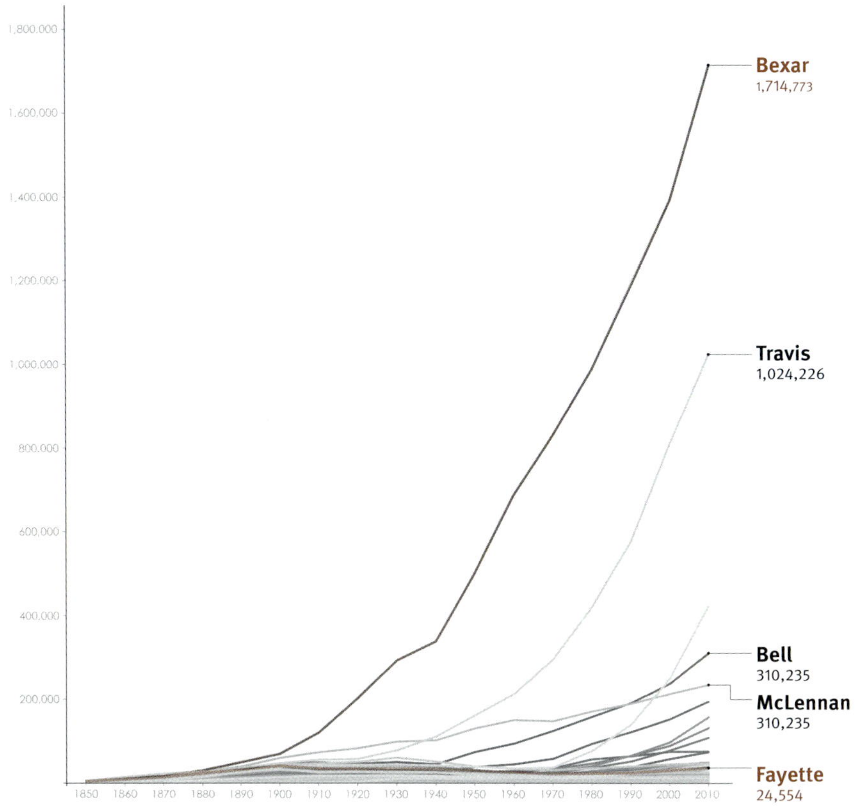

Central Texas population, 1850–2010

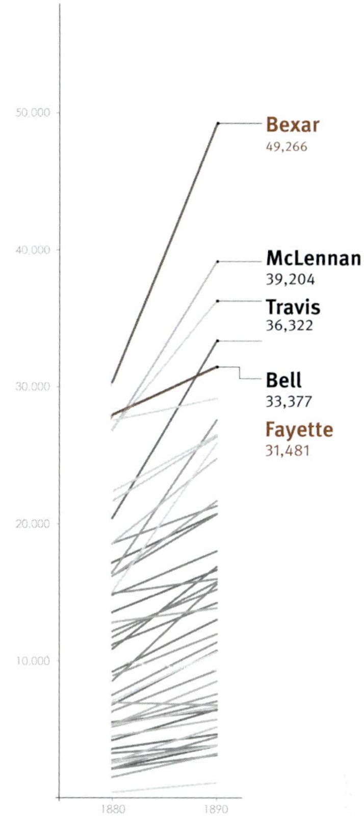

Central Texas population, 1890

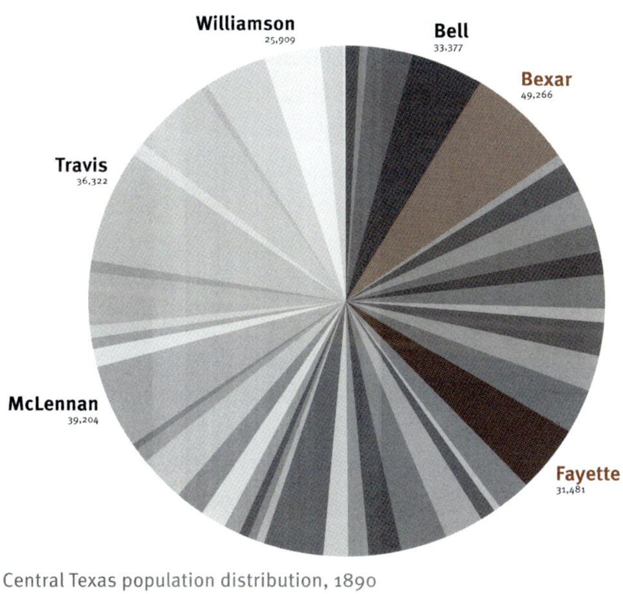

Central Texas population distribution, 1890

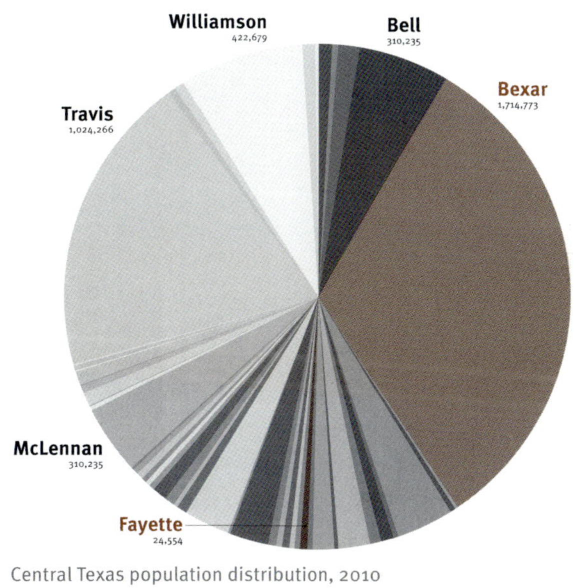

Central Texas population distribution, 2010

Hays County Courthouse, 1908, San Marcos, Texas

grants, booming cotton production, and the arrival of the Galveston, Harrisburg, and San Antonio Railroad only a few years before, the county had many factors working in its favor. Community leaders understandably wanted to encourage additional growth, and at the time, an ambitious courthouse was seen as a catalyst for economic development. As well as raising property values for real estate directly adjacent to it, a monumental courthouse acted as tangible proof of a county's stability and prosperity. Just as a new Wal-Mart spurred development in the closing decades of the twentieth century, a robust new courthouse could inspire equivalent development at the end of the nineteenth. Thus, the construction of an architecturally ambitious county courthouse should not be viewed as a reckless act of governmental extravagance but rather as a direct investment in the future prosperity of a community. By designing for the future they wanted, rather than in reaction to the present that existed, counties provided themselves with buildings that acted as constant physical reminders of the ideals that would propel their communities forward. They still do this today.

ON GOVERNMENT

In the latter half of the nineteenth century the wounds of the Civil War remained fresh. Although the causes of the war were complex, the conflict ultimately was fought to resolve a fundamental question about government. As Abraham Lincoln memorably stated, his task was to preserve the union so that a *government* of the people, by the people, and for the people would not perish from the earth.

This was not merely a politician's rhetorical spin on a contentious issue. Rather, it was a commonly held understanding of the war that was shared by rank and file citizens and soldiers.[1] In both the North and the South, differing understandings about the authority of state government—especially as it related to slavery—were seen as the primary cause of the war. This provides some insight into why, a few decades later, sparsely populated counties in central Texas invested so many material and financial resources into the construction of government office buildings. If the reach of the federal government was worth dying on the battlefield to define, surely local government was worth celebrating on the courthouse square.

It is important to remember that the wholesale distrust of the institution of government is a relatively modern phenomenon.[2] Historically, Americans had great confidence in the system of government established by the Constitution. To disparage that government would be to decry one of the defining characteristics of the American experiment. This began to change significantly in the twentieth century, when a growing distrust began to develop of government in all its forms.[3] Although nearly three-quarters of Americans felt they could trust their government as recently as the early 1960s, by 1980 that ratio had reversed, with three-quarters expressing the belief that their government could *not* be trusted.[4]

With so much political discourse today framed by antigovernment rhetoric, the notion of a public building celebrating the institution of government seems absurd. Though it may be difficult to measure objectively, there can be little doubt that the attitude toward government that inspired the construction of the grand courthouses of a century ago is radically different from the cynical one that now pervades American society. Today, government in Texas is expected to be as minimal and efficient as possible, and the architecture that is created to house it more often than not reflects that shift in public sentiment. In this context, the courthouses of a century ago exist as foreign artifacts from a time when priorities were very different.

ON PRESERVATION

In the decades that followed their construction, many courthouses fell into increasing states of disrepair. Designed to meet the programmatic needs that existed at a specific time, these buildings often proved difficult to adapt to the changing scope of county government. Years of deferred maintenance, poor integration of updated mechanical systems, and insensitive remodeling efforts all took a destructive toll.

The most nefarious threat to the survival of a historic county courthouse in the twentieth century was not fire or neglect but the prosperity and rapid growth of the county itself. When courthouses were not replaced outright, the need for expanded facilities often resulted in hastily built additions that severely compromised the buildings' original architectural intent. The 1930s were a particularly dangerous time, when federal funds became available to subsidize significant alterations to or replacements of existing courthouses. Although this work was motivated by legitimate functional or structural deficiencies, the results were often disastrous for the integrity of a building's original design. Towers and domes were removed, and cornices and other architectural ornamentation were eliminated in aggressive aesthetic "modernizations."

By 1998 the situation across Texas had deteriorated to the point that the National Trust for Historic Preservation took the remarkable step of placing Texas' county courthouses as a group on its annual list of Most Endangered Historic Places in the United States.[5] Public sentiment almost universally favored returning these structures to their original conditions, but local budget realities often limited the scale of restoration work that could be afforded. Although stopgap measures could be undertaken, the radical interventions that many courthouses by then required were beyond the means of most counties.

In 1999 the Texas Legislature created and funded the Texas Historic Courthouse Preservation Program (THCPP). Championed by then-governor George W. Bush, the program charged the Texas Historical Commission with administering a process by which counties could apply for and receive matching state grants to execute appropriate restoration work. In the years that have passed since its inception, the results of the program have been profound. As of 2014, 180 grants have been awarded to ninety-six counties. A total of fifty-nine courthouses have been fully restored with the assistance of THCPP grants.

The act of preservation is an important and noble endeavor. The sustained efforts of all involved parties—county taxpayers, commissioners courts, historical societies as well as the Texas Historical Commission, preservation architects, contractors, and craftspeople—have ensured that a key part of the state's architectural legacy will be perpetuated for generations to come. Yet preserving a courthouse is not without its curious side effects. Often obscured in the process of restoring a courthouse to an earlier historical appearance is any evidence of the building's less-than-idyllic past. It should be remembered that racial segregation was firmly institutionalized in Texas at the time the state was constructing its finest courthouses. The courts that were held in these structures adjudicated the same Jim Crow laws that kept generations of African Americans and other minorities politically, economically, and socially isolated. These buildings were designed to reinforce this status quo as well. Courtrooms with segregated balconies and "colored only" restrooms and water fountains provided architecturally separate facilities for their nonwhite visitors.

Although the Texas Historical Commission encourages counties to document and interpret these chapters from their past, many choose not to do so. Although the literal reinstallation of segregated facilities would of course be problematic, their total elimination ultimately represents a kind of historical sugarcoating that downplays a significant part of the state's complex history.

The collision of the honorable goals of historic preservation with the realities of modern use is prominently displayed in other ways in even the most sensitively restored courthouses. Preserving grand exterior stairs leading to an elevated first floor is challenging when accessibility standards require wheelchair access. Maintaining multiple entries into a courthouse is problematic when security needs require visitors to pass through bulky metal detectors. Perpetuating the architectural presence of a courthouse on a square is impossible when the small saplings planted a century ago have grown into towering trees that obscure the building in its entirety.

It would be difficult to argue convincingly for the removal of hundred-year-old oaks in the name of "preservation," but these conundrums illustrate the fact that courthouses remain dynamic entities that resist any attempt to remain static. Just as the trees planted in their squares continue to grow, county courthouses and the governments they house continue to evolve. The best way to preserve them is to ensure that counties have the flexibility and funding to adapt to changing demands.

ON MOVING FORWARD

As compelling as the courthouses of central Texas may be, they are products of a time and a culture that no longer exists. In the century between when construction began on the courthouse in Kendall County and when the new courthouse in Zavala County opened its doors, Texas evolved from a patchwork of poor and widely dispersed agricultural communities into a wealthy, high-tech economy centered in a few sprawling metropolises. This transition was not

View of Mason County Courthouse, circa 1953, Mason, Texas. Photo courtesy of the Texas Department of Transportation

View of Mason County Courthouse, 2013, Mason, Texas

Coryell County Courthouse, 1897, Gatesville, Texas

painless. The conflicting values of the state's rural past and its urban future continue to spur cultural as well as legislative debate.

Apart from the transformation of the society that commissioned these courthouses, the manner in which that architecture was built changed as well. The original Kendall County Courthouse did not have electricity or indoor plumbing when it was constructed in 1870. A century later, the Zavala County Courthouse enjoyed sophisticated mechanical, electrical, and telecommunications systems. Even if architects today were to choose to replicate the designs of bygone eras, due to fundamental changes in construction practices and performance expectations, their attempts to resurrect the architecture of the nineteenth century using contemporary building techniques would result in mere simulations of the originals. The endeavor would also be outrageously expensive.

The point of this study is not to advocate a return to an Italianate or Romanesque mode of design. The existence of modern architecture cannot be ignored any more than can the centuries of historic architecture that came before it. But although they do not provide an explicit way forward, the courthouses of central Texas do provide relevant lessons for contemporary architects. They prove that there is a place for grandeur in public buildings. Just as a judge dons a robe to signify his or her legal authority, courthouse buildings adopted formal conventions to reinforce the social importance of the institution they housed.

Perhaps more importantly, the courthouses of central Texas demonstrate that good architecture cannot exist in a vacuum. Communities throughout central Texas found symbolic and economic reasons to build as financing tools became available that allowed their expanding economies to afford such structures. Skilled but inexpensive immigrant labor helped make these construction projects affordable as did an expanding rail transportation network. Had Texas been settled a few decades later or urbanized a few decades earlier, the resulting courthouses would have been very different. The built artifacts that exist today represent a perfect alignment of multiple variables that all favored the construction of good courthouse buildings.

Although most Texas county courthouses are handsome structures, it is not their beauty alone that endears them to us. It is not their setting in a landscaped square, nor is it the towers or domes that rise above their roofs. It is the fact that they provide an appropriately public center for their communities. It is the fact they are so unabashedly optimistic. It is the fact they speak to a government that is approachable, a society that is progressive, and a future that is brighter. They tell us in a clear and resonant voice that, when we listen to the better angels of our nature, we can together build a better world.

Washington County Courthouse, 1939, Brenham, Texas

Acknowledgments

Although my name may be the one that appears on the cover of this book, many others played a role in its creation. Some are close friends and family members who helped me along the way, while others are scholars whom I have never met but whose work provided the foundation for this study.

The astute reader will notice that I relied heavily on secondary sources for the portions of the text that give historical context to the courthouses of central Texas. I did this not out of intellectual laziness, but because the existing scholarship is so strong. Willard Robinson's *The People's Architecture* should be considered the starting point for any study of public buildings in Texas. Published after his untimely death, Robert Veselka's *The Courthouse Square in Texas* is a remarkable analysis of the relationship of courthouse buildings to their urban contexts. Many of the studies I undertook as part of my project are graphic extensions of observations made in Veselka's work. Chris Meister's essays in *Southwestern Historical Quarterly* tell some of the more fascinating stories of Texas courthouses. His *James Riely Gordon: His Courthouses and Other Public Architecture* is now *the* source for information on Gordon, and I have referenced it several times in my work here. Chris also provided assistance in verifying sources and reconstructing elevations of long since demolished Gordon courthouses.

A number of other books have served as valuable references as well. *The Texas Courthouse* and *Courthouses of Texas* are two survey books that contain photographs and information about all 254 courthouse buildings in the state. The former volume, by June Rayfield and Larry Nance, is in many ways a time capsule, describing the state of these buildings as of 1971. The latter effort, by Mavis Kelsey and Donald Dyal, provides updated color imagery and also contains a number of introductory essays that reveal a depth of understanding that can only come from years of dedicated research and observation. When seen in context with the earlier volume, it also vividly illustrates the transformative results of the state's preservation efforts as well as some of the courthouses that have unfortunately been lost.

Although most of the courthouses surveyed are now over a hundred years old, I conducted my research on them in the twenty-first century and took full advantage of the technologies available to me. Satellite imagery was helpful in creating the courthouse square diagrams seen throughout this study and in better understanding the relationship these buildings have to their urban environments. The aerial photography was made possible by consumer-grade, unmanned aerial vehicles that have become affordable to individual researchers such as myself only in the last few years. Computational fluid dynamic modeling has similarly become available as a practical tool for analysis only recently, although it still requires engineering and computing skills that I do not possess. I am indebted to Nishant Kanapilly and Kelly Scott, of Cleary Zimmermann Engineers, who ran the simulations necessary for me to say that the towers on Gordon's courthouses did much more than just look good.

I also owe a special thanks to the students who endured my design studio at the University of Texas at Austin. The early precedent studies they executed in the fall of 2008 in many ways represent the starting point for this project.

Jelisa Blumberg and Kristin Walsh also provided helpful early assistance in analyzing data and imagining how it might be effectively conveyed. Katy Silva performed important last-minute checking of dates and spellings.

Readers of early drafts of the manuscript of this book provided incredibly useful feedback and helped refine a sprawling mass of disjointed observations into something more focused. Richard Cleary, Max Levy, and Michael Malone provided encouragement and engaging conversation about the initial direction of this project. Max also generously agreed to write the foreword of this book. My only regret in having him do this is that the poetry of his writing makes everything that follows read like mediocre prose at best.

Jay Louden, Raina Tilden, and Luke Johnson all provided important feedback on later versions of the manuscript, while Chris Meister and Mark Cowan applied their encyclopedic knowledge of courthouses to identify and eliminate errors that made their way into the developing manuscript. Mark, a project reviewer at the Texas Historical Commission, was incredibly patient with my constant barrage of questions. Sharon Fleming, also of the THC, similarly provided her time, knowledge, and encouragement. Jon Carroll, an attorney who happens to also be my cousin, helped explain to me the intricacies of the Texas legal system. Stephen Sharpe, who for years was my editor at *Texas Architect*, turned his critical eye to this project and helped tighten my prose and curtail my pervasive use of the passive voice. Erica Goranson suffered through both early and later drafts of the manuscript and helped make sure I was actually making a cohesive argument. Stephen Fox provided critical assistance in the final polishing of the text, and Julie Pizzo Wood lent a critical eye to the graphics.

Of course, no one would be reading any of this if not for the University of Texas Press. I am grateful for the trust and opportunity afforded by them and the skill and dedication of their staff. I am especially indebted to Jim Burr, my sponsoring editor, who held my hand through the two and a half year process that ultimately resulted in this volume's publication. Along the way, Ellen McKie helped transform a pile of words and images into a real book.

And no list of acknowledgments is complete without a nod to the support of my family. My parents instilled in me a love of books that no doubt was the genesis of my desire to pen one of my own. My wife, Clara, has not only been permissive of my unending need to travel to towns she has never heard of, but she is also an extraordinary copy editor who refuses to indulge my desire to overuse commas. My first daughter, Sammy, was born around the same time I began dedicated work on this project, and the two will forever be intertwined in my memory. And although my second daughter, Darcy, came along as work was winding down, she and her sister both helped me keep things in perspective while allowing me to see the world for the truly remarkable place that it is.

Finally, a debt of gratitude is owed to the architects who dedicated years of their professional careers to the restoration of the courthouses included in this study. In addition to executing their preservation work, they also provided me with technical assistance and encouragement throughout the development of this project. In many cases I used their drawings to verify the measurements and observations I made in the field.

Although many more architects have worked on courthouses throughout the state, the following firms helped make this particular project possible:

Architects Rabe + Partners
4201 Bee Cave Road, Building C, Suite 201
Austin, Texas 78746
512.349.7173

ARCHITEXAS
2900 South Congress Avenue
Austin, Texas 78704
512.444.4220

Arthur Weinman Architects
6300 Ridglea Place, Suite 105
Fort Worth, Texas 76116
817.737.0977

Bailey Architects
55 Waugh Drive, Suite 450
Houston, Texas 77007
713.524.2155

DMS Architects
300 College Avenue
Fort Worth, Texas 76104
817.570.2000

1113 Architects
1506 South Elm Street
Georgetown, Texas 78626
512.869.1104

Fisher Heck Architects, Inc.
915 South Saint Mary's Street
San Antonio, Texas 78205
210.299.1500

Komatsu Architecture
3880 Hulen Street, Suite 300
Fort Worth, Texas 76107
817.332.1914

Lord Aeck Sargent
3636 Executive Center Drive, Suite 254
Austin, Texas 78731
512.346.8546

Norman Alston Architects
400 North Ervay Street, Suite 212
Dallas, Texas 75201
214.826.5466

Kim Williams, Architect
(formerly The Williams Company, AIA, and TWC Architects)
P.O. Box 27294
Austin, Texas 78755
512.940.4755

Volz O'Connell Hutson Architecture and Interior Design
(formerly Volz & Associates)
1105 West 42nd Street
Austin, Texas 78756
512.476.0433

Barry A. Wagner, Architect and Preservation Consultant
(formerly Wagner and Klein, Architects and Preservation Consultants)
508 North Milam Street
Fredericksburg, Texas 78624
830.997.9525

Sinclair & Wright Architects
320 S Broadway Avenue
Tyler, Texas 75702
903.595.2656

Gonzales County Courthouse, 1894, Gonzales, Texas

Notes

INTRODUCTION

1. Alexander Caragonne, *The Texas Rangers: Notes from an Architectural Underground* (Cambridge, MA: MIT Press, 1995), 249.

2. Colin Rowe and John Hejduk, "Lockhart, Texas," *Architectural Record* 121 (March 1957): 201–206.

3. All population figures used in this study reflect United States Census data.

4. Robert E. Veselka, *The Courthouse Square in Texas*, ed. Kenneth E. Foote (Austin: University of Texas Press, 2000), 9.

5. Although little original architectural documentation survives, the Texas Historical Commission has assembled an impressive collection of building data for its Texas Historic Courthouse Preservation Program. In order for a county to receive a matching state grant, the commission requires the production of a master plan outlining the existing condition of the courthouse and defining the scope of the proposed restorative work. These documents were executed by many of the leading preservation firms in the state, and the drawings created for them were referenced to verify the field measurements made at the courthouses themselves. A list of these architects can be found in the acknowledgments.

CHAPTER 1: THE COUNTY COURTHOUSE

1. Christopher S. Davies, "Life at the Edge: Urban and Industrial Evolution of Texas, Frontier Wilderness—Frontier Space, 1836–1986," *Southwestern Historical Quarterly* 89, no. 4 (1986): 486.

2. June Rayfield Welch and J. Larry Nance, *The Texas Courthouse* (Dallas: G. L. A. Press, 1971), 1–2.

3. Seymour V. Connor, "The Evolution of County Government in the Republic of Texas," *Southwestern Historical Quarterly* 55, no. 2 (1951): 199.

4. The school superintendent was once a county official, but public schools are now operated in Texas within independent districts.

5. Edward T. Price, "The Central Courthouse Square in the American County Seat," *Geographical Review* 58, no. 1 (1968): 29.

6. Willard B. Robinson, *The People's Architecture: Texas Courthouses, Jails, and Municipal Buildings* (Austin: Texas State Historical Association, 1983), 19.

7. Ibid., 36.

8. See Kerr and Washington Counties.

9. Robert E. Veselka, *The Courthouse Square in Texas*, ed. Kenneth E. Foote (Austin: University of Texas Press, 2000), 172.

10. Price, "Central Courthouse Square," 42–52. In *The Courthouse Square in Texas*, Robert Veselka refined the definitions established by Price and made them specific to Texas.

11. Mavis P. Kelsey and Donald H. Dyal, *The Courthouses of Texas*, 2nd ed. (College Station: Texas A&M University Press, 2007), xvi.

12. Willard Robinson's *The People's Architecture* provides an obvious starting point for any discussion of public buildings in Texas. A sprawling history of courthouses, city halls, and jails, it provides the foundation for much of the historical background provided in this section.

13. Robinson, *The People's Architecture*, 47–52.

14. Ibid., 127.

15. Willard B. Robinson, "The Public Square as a Determinant of Courthouse Form in Texas," *Southwestern Historical Quarterly* 75, no. 3 (1971): 345.

16. Jay C. Henry, *Architecture in Texas: 1895–1945* (Austin: University of Texas Press, 1993), 26.

17. Cleary Zimmermann Engineers of San Antonio performed computational fluid dynamic simulations on the Comal County Courthouse on behalf of the author to determine the effectiveness of the passive cooling systems of these buildings as originally configured. Thermal comfort is determined by many different factors including both the temperature of the air and its perceived movement. With exterior windows and interior doors fully open, air moved through the building at 150 feet per minute. This would be experienced as an almost imperceptible breeze—great enough to cool but not be felt as a draft. Combined with an air temperature in the upper seventies, this would be considered comfortable by contemporary standards.

As a side note, after the windows of the courthouse had been removed as part of the 2012 restoration, workers reported how the building's design augmented the circulation of air and thus the structure effectively cooled itself.

18. Welch and Nance, *The Texas Courthouse*, 9.

19. Martin Greif, *Depression Modern: The Thirties Style in America* (New York: Universe, 1975).

20. Robinson, *The People's Architecture*, 264–269.

21. Davies, “Life at the Edge,” 481.

22. Welch and Nance, *The Texas Courthouse*, 9.

CHAPTER 2: THE COURTHOUSES OF CENTRAL TEXAS

1. The Robertson County Courthouse was in the process of being restored as the final version of this manuscript was being assembled, so the elevation and plan drawings illustrated here are based on the architects' drawings rather than on field measurements. A special thinks to Sinclair and Wright Architects for making their original drawings available.

2. The building is still in use in theory. In 2011 the Wilson County Courthouse was determined to be unsafe and evacuated by county officials. As of late 2014, it is still awaiting restoration.

3. The Bell County Courthouse was designed and constructed while the Texas State Capitol was being built. The Capitol, too, was originally intended to have a square dome, although a more traditional hemispherical dome was ultimately constructed. Unlike that of the State Capitol, the dome of the Bell County Courthouse was removed before being replaced as part of the building's 1999 restoration.

4. Although the original Hamilton County Courthouse closely resembles courthouses by Ruffini and other contemporaries, the designer of the 1886 structure is uncertain. No architect is listed on the cornerstone, and the historical records are incomplete.

5. The Fannin and Tyler County Courthouses have also been extensively modified but have yet to be restored to their original conditions.

6. The partnership of Larmour and Watson was dissolved during the Llano County project, and this perhaps explains why only Watson's name appears on the cornerstone.

7. The original tower closely resembled the one in Bandera County and may have been based on the same set of drawings. Such borrowing by architects and contractors was more common when photography was less common and intellectual property rights were less developed.

8. An almost identical copy of the Milam County Courthouse was built in Comanche County at the same time, although that building was replaced by the current structure in 1939.

9. There exists some confusion concerning the authorship of both the Caldwell County Courthouse and its sister in Goliad County. Although they are often attributed to Alfred Giles, Henry Guindon was in all likelihood the originator of the designs. Guindon's periodic professional affiliation with Giles leads to these projects often being attributed to the better known San Antonio architect.

10. Or at least they are nearly identical now. In 1942 a hurricane destroyed the towers of the Goliad Courthouse. The structure remained decapitated for sixty-two years, until they were rebuilt in 2003.

11. Fisher Heck Architects, Inc., and Graham B Luhn Architects have both contributed to this restoration effort.

12. A more typical configuration can be found in Mason County, where the courthouse is centered in the enlarged square so as to align with the street interrupted by the square.

13. As of late 2014, Fisher Heck Architects, Inc., and Alamo Architects are conducting ongoing interior and exterior restoration work.

14. Dodson's more typical approach to courthouse design can be seen in Hill and Lampasas Counties.

15. While formally similar, these buildings are quite different when seen in person and are different in color because of their different exterior material palettes.

16. Gordon had already changed his stylistic approach, as can be seen in his contemporary design for the McLennan County Courthouse.

17. The 1882 Robertson County Courthouse was remodeled in 1924 to have its Second-Empire cornice and roofline replaced with one more mission-like in appearance. In 2014 it was returned to its original appearance, leaving Atascosa as the sole mission-style courthouse in central Texas.

18. Blanco still has the old Blanco County Courthouse sitting in the middle of town. The 1885 structure was designed by F. E. Ruffini and has been well maintained since it was decommissioned, although a suitable purpose for the building has yet to be found.

19. See the elevation studies of Lee and Burleson Counties, pp. 141–142.

20. When it was completed, the project received national coverage, culminating in a feature article in the January 1957 issue of *Architectural Record*.

21. Portions of these original corridors have been filled in over time to accommodate the need for expanded office and storage space.

22. Willard B. Robinson, *The People's Architecture: Texas Courthouses, Jails, and Municipal Buildings* (Austin: Texas State Historical Association, 1983), 121–123.

23. The elaborate towers of Dodson's designs clearly reference John McArthur's Philadelphia City Hall. Although that project

was not completed until 1901, construction had begun in 1871, and Dodson was no doubt familiar with the competition-winning design.

24. An expanded version of this section first appeared as "The Curious Case of James Riely Gordon," *Pidgin* 14 (2012): 162–177.

25. Gordon's completed Texas courthouse projects are here arranged chronologically by date of completion, with the exception of the project in Bexar County. Although this project was not completed until 1896, it was designed in 1891. The projects identified as "reconstructed" were drawn with information gleaned from existing historical drawings, photos, and descriptions. Chris Meister was an invaluable resource in this effort.

CONCLUSIONS

1. Sullivan Ballou, a major in the U.S. Army during the Civil War, stated as much when he wrote a now-famous letter to his wife. In it he said he knew "how strongly American Civilization now leans upon the triumph of the Government, and how great a debt we owe to those who went before us through the blood and suffering of the Revolution." He added, "And I am willing—perfectly willing—to lay down all my joys in this life, to help maintain this Government, and to pay that debt." Notice how Ballou states that he is fighting to preserve not freedom or liberty but "the government."

2. Stephen Earl Bennett, "Were the Halcyon Days Really Golden? An Analysis of Americans' Attitudes about the Political System, 1945–1965," in *What Is It about Government That Americans Dislike?*, ed. John R. Hibbing and Elizabeth Theiss-Morse (New York: Cambridge University Press, 2001), 48–49.

3. Amy Fried and Douglas B. Harris, "On Red Capes and Charging Bulls: How and Why Conservative Politicians and Interest Groups Promoted Public Anger," in Hibbing and Theiss-Morse, *What Is It about Government That Americans Dislike?*, 158–159.

4. John R. Alford, "We're All in This Together: The Decline of Trust in Government, 1958–1996," in Hibbing and Theiss-Morse, *What Is It about Government That Americans Dislike?*, 30–31.

5. The historic courthouses of Texas were again placed on the National Trust for Historic Preservation's list of most endangered places in 2012. Despite the success of the program over the previous decade, the Texas Legislature increasingly cut funds to the program in subsequent legislative sessions. This resulted in a growing backlog of courthouses that qualified for assistance but could not be funded. Although the program remains popular, in 2013 the Texas Legislature further reduced funding of the program to $4.5 million, less than a tenth of the $50 million the program was budgeted in the early years of its existence.

Grimes County Courthouse, 1893, Anderson, Texas

Bibliography

Alford, John R. "We're All in This Together: The Decline of Trust in Government, 1958–1996." In *What Is It about Government That Americans Dislike?*, edited by John R. Hibbing and Elizabeth Theiss-Morse, 28–46. New York: Cambridge University Press, 2001.

Bennett, Stephen Earl. "Were the Halcyon Days Really Golden? An Analysis of Americans' Attitudes about the Political System, 1945–1965." In *What Is It about Government That Americans Dislike?*, edited by John R. Hibbing and Elizabeth Theiss-Morse, 47–58. New York: Cambridge University Press, 2001.

Breich, Kenneth A. "The Richardsonian Interlude in Texas: A Quest for Meaning and Order at the End of the Nineteenth Century." In *The Spirit of H. H. Richardson on the Midland Prairies*, edited by Paul Clifford Larson and Susan M. Brown, 87–105. Ames: Iowa State University, 1988.

Burka, Paul. "Farmers Flight!" *Texas Monthly*, November 2011.

Caragonne, Alexander. *The Texas Rangers: Notes from an Architectural Underground*. Cambridge, MA: MIT Press, 1995.

Connor, Seymour V. "The Evolution of County Government in the Republic of Texas." *Southwestern Historical Quarterly* 55, no. 2 (1951): 163–200.

Davies, Christopher S. "Life at the Edge: Urban and Industrial Evolution of Texas, Frontier Wilderness—Frontier Space, 1836–1986." *Southwestern Historical Quarterly* 89, no. 4 (1986): 443–554.

Fried, Amy, and Douglas B. Harris. "On Red Capes and Charging Bulls: How and Why Conservative Politicians and Interest Groups Promoted Public Anger." In *What Is It about Government That Americans Dislike?*, edited by John R. Hibbing and Elizabeth Theiss-Morse, 157–174. New York: Cambridge University Press, 2001.

Gournay, Luke. *Texas Boundaries: Evolution of the State's Counties*. College Station: Texas A&M University Press, 1995.

Greif, Martin. *Depression Modern: The Thirties Style in America*. New York: Universe, 1975.

Hall, Michael. "Paper Chase." *Texas Monthly*, February 2012.

Henry, Jay C. *Architecture in Texas: 1895–1945*. Austin: University of Texas Press, 1993.

———. "The Richardsonian Romanesque in Texas." *Texas Architect* 31, no. 1 (1981): 52–59.

Hitchcock, Henry-Russell, and William Seale. "Notes on the Architecture." In *Court House: A Photographic Document*, edited by Richard Pare, 165–250. New York: Horizon, 1978.

Jackson, John Brinckerhoff. "The Almost Perfect Town." In *Landscape in Sight: Looking at America*, edited by Helen Lefkowitz Horowitz, 31–42. New Haven, CT: Yale University Press, 1997.

———. "The Necessity for Ruins." In *The Necessity for Ruins, and Other Topics*, 89–102. Amherst: University of Massachusetts Press, 1980.

Kelsey, Mavis P., and Donald H. Dyal. *The Courthouses of Texas*. 2nd ed. College Station: Texas A&M University Press, 2007.

Lambert, Phyllis. "The Record of Building as Evidence." In *Court House: A Photographic Document*, edited by Richard Pare, 10–13. New York: Horizon, 1978.

Meister, Chris. *James Riely Gordon: His Courthouses and Other Public Architecture*. Lubbock: Texas Tech University Press, 2011.

Pare, Richard. Introduction to *Court House: A Photographic Document*, edited by Richard Pare, 7–9. New York: Horizon, 1978.

Price, Edward T. "The Central Courthouse Square in the American County Seat." *Geographical Review* 58, no. 1 (1968): 29–60.

Robinson, Willard B. "The Public Square as a Determinant of Courthouse Form in Texas." *Southwestern Historical Quarterly* 75, no. 3 (1971): 339–384.

———. *The People's Architecture: Texas Courthouses, Jails, and Municipal Buildings*. Austin: Texas State Historical Association, 1983.

Rowe, Colin, and John Hejduk. "Lockhart, Texas." *Architectural Record* 121 (March 1957): 201–206.

Silverstein, Vivian. "The Law and James Riely Gordon." *Texas Bar Journal* 45, no. 9 (1982): 1306–1309.

Sullivan, Louis. *The Autobiography of an Idea*. Rev. ed. New York: Dover, 1956.

Veselka, Robert E. *The Courthouse Square in Texas*. Edited by Kenneth E. Foote. Austin: University of Texas Press, 2000.

"Vestiges of Segregation Removed." *Los Angeles Times*, September 12, 2003.

Welch, June Rayfield, and J. Larry Nance. *The Texas Courthouse*. Dallas: G. L. A. Press, 1971.

Bosque County Courthouse, 1886, Meridian, Texas

Index

A boldface page range indicates the principal discussion of a courthouse.

NAILHEAD SPUR CO

ATASCOSA

BANDERA

BASTROP

BELL

BEXAR

CALDWELL

COMAL

COMANCHE

CORYELL

FALLS

GRIMES

GUADALUPE

HAMILTON

HAYS

HILL

LEON

LIMESTONE

LLANO

MCCULLOCH

MCLENNAN

NAVARRO

REAL

ROBERTSON

SAN SABA

TRAVIS

BLANCO

BOSQUE

BRAZOS

BURLESON

BURNET

FAYETTE

FREESTONE

FRIO

GILLESPIE

GONZALES

KARNES

KENDALL

KERR

LAMPASAS

LEE

MADISON

MASON

MEDINA

MILAM

MILLS

UVALDE

WASHINGTON

WILLIAMSON

WILSON

ZAVALA